D1516808

WILLIAM BUTLER YEATS

# JOHN SHERMAN

# &

# DHOYA

THE TATE GALLERY, LONDON

*W. B. Yeats* (1907) *by Augustus John*
*reproduced by kind permission of Mrs. Augustus John.*

WILLIAM BUTLER YEATS

# JOHN SHERMAN

# &

# DHOYA

*edited, with an introduction, collation*
*of the texts, and notes by*
Richard J. Finneran
NEW YORK UNIVERSITY

*Wayne State University Press, Detroit, 1969*

Edward Miner Gallaudet Memorial Library

Copyright © 1969 by Wayne State University Press,
Detroit, Michigan 48202, exclusive of the following
copyrights:

*John Sherman* and *Dhoya* copyright 1891 by W. B.
Yeats. The present edition copyright 1969 by Anne
Yeats and Michael Butler Yeats and reprinted with
their express permission.

All rights are reserved. No part of this book may
be reproduced without formal permission.

Published simultaneously in Canada
by The Copp Clark Publishing Company
517 Wellington Street, West
Toronto 2B, Canada.

Library of Congress Catalog Card Number: 69–14424
Standard Book Number: 8143–1389–2

823.8
Y43j
1969

# Contents

121830

# Preface

*This edition has* been made possible primarily by two people, both of whom have been most generous in their assistance. In the first place I would like to thank Mr. Michael B. Yeats, who not only obtained the kind permission of the late Mrs. W. B. Yeats for the republication of *John Sherman and Dhoya* but also provided me with detailed answers to the constant stream of questions with which I was forced to trouble him. His skillful administration of the literary estate of W. B. Yeats is an important contribution to Anglo-Irish scholarship—as I am sure all those who have worked on Yeats know.

Dr. George Mills Harper had no less an influence on this edition. It was Dr. Harper who first gave my interest in Yeats a firm direction, suggesting, in fact, the original concept of this book. His assistance ranges from an introduction to Mr. Yeats at the Yeats International Summer School at Sligo in 1964 to learned and valuable comments on the manuscript. Both his encouragement as a friend and advice as a scholar have been invaluable.

Two other people have made contributions to this edition which are perhaps smaller but nevertheless irreplaceable. Professor Brendan P. O Hehir has given generously of his time in providing me with translations of the Gaelic words in the text. His replies to my questions have always been exhaustive. Mrs. Sheelah Kirby has also been most helpful in matters relating to Yeats's use of the Sligo area. Her knowledge of Sligo geography, traditions, and legends has made clear a number of obscure matters.

Other debts which I have incurred can only be briefly mentioned here: Mrs. Daphne Fullwood, Dr. T. R. Henn, and Miss Virginia Moore for their kind assistance in my effort to locate the allusion to a French writer on magic; Professors Richard Harter Fogle, Fred C. Thompson, and Weldon Thornton for their comments on the manuscript; the Smith Fund of the University of North Carolina for a grant to aid in the purchase of needed microfilms; The Placenames Commission of the Ordnance Survey Office in Dublin for their help; and the Libraries of the University of North Carolina and the University of Florida.

Finally, I would like to dedicate my work on this edition to Maude Florence Finneran—who, in other ways, indeed made it all possible.

R. J. F.

# Introduction

## Composition and Publication History

*Sometime in what* must have been 1887, John Butler Yeats is said to have suggested that his son William write a prose story, "partly of London, partly of Sligo."[1]* In a letter to Katharine Tynan in 1887 (probably, according to Allan Wade, August 13th), Yeats noted that he "was resolved to try story-writing but so far [had] not made a start."[2] Apparently he soon began, however, for in a letter written in the autumn of 1887 he speaks of *Dhoya*, the first result of his father's remark, as in a finished or near-finished form.[3] In December of that year he sent the story to John O'Leary for possible inclusion in the *Gael*, "hoping it may suit for the Xmas number, for some number anyway."[4] Although the lack of any extant file of the *Gael* makes certainty impossible, it is quite unlikely that the story appeared there: Yeats nowhere makes mention of a separate publication of *Dhoya*, and the *Gael* itself was suspended in January, 1888.[5]

The single setting of Sligo which Yeats employed in

* Superscript numbers in the Introduction refer to notes located at the back of the book.

*Dhoya* obviously did not meet his father's stipulation; and, at any rate, John Butler Yeats told his son that he had "meant a story about real people."[6] Dutifully, Yeats set to work on what was to become *John Sherman*. He wrote Katharine Tynan in February of 1888 that he would soon "set to work at a short romance."[7] Two months later he was "reading up" for his "romance," planning to set it in the "eighteenth century."[8] By May of 1888 Yeats was actually at work on the story, and in June he stated that "another chapter will finish it."[9]

At this point, however, Yeats had to postpone his work on *John Sherman* to make a copy for Alfred Nutt of a rare Aesop manuscript at the Bodleian: "My story waits for its last chapter and will have to wait till immediate work concludes."[10] It was not until October that he was able to inform John O'Leary that "the first draft is complete."[11] Although a month later *John Sherman* was "being rewritten in the latter parts,"[12] by the end of 1888 the story was completed.[13]

Yeats's attentions in 1889 were focused on many different areas—Maud Gonne and the editing of Blake being but two—and he seems to have given little thought in that year to either *John Sherman* or *Dhoya*. He did, though, express some dissatisfaction with the former in a letter to Katharine Tynan on April 21, 1889: "I know I gained greatly from my experiment in novel writing. The hero turned out a bad character and so I did not try to sell the story anywhere. I am in hopes he may reform."[14] But by October, 1890, Yeats had changed his mind and was attempting to find a publisher for *John Sherman*: he told Miss Tynan that he had "retouched" the story and was "trying to get it published."[15]

Through the good offices of Edward Garnett, *John Sherman* was accepted by T. Fisher Unwin in March of 1891 for his Pseudonym Library series. The story went to the press in June of that year, Yeats in the meantime having decided to include *Dhoya*—which was then variously entitled *The Midnight Ride* or *The Midnight Rider*.[16]

Thus, in November of 1891 two thousand copies of *John Sherman and Dhoya* by "Ganconagh" were published as the tenth number of Unwin's Pseudonym Library.[17] Coming after the earlier *Mosada* (1886) and *The Wanderings of Oisin* (1889), it was but the third separate publication of Yeats's work.

One must pause here to note that the use of a pseudonym ("Ganconagh," meaning "love-talker," is the name of an Irish fairy) was the idea of the publisher and not Yeats: "Unwin I believe makes rather a point of the Pseudonymous nature of the books," he wrote John O'Leary.[18] However, the poem included in *Dhoya* had already been published under the title of "Girl's Song" in *The Wanderings of Oisin*; therefore, as Yeats informed Katharine Tynan, the "incognito" was "pretty transparent."[19] Indeed, when he sent a review copy to Father Matthew Russell, the editor of the *Irish Monthly*, Yeats stated that "I want it to be known as mine."[20]

Regardless of its anonymous publication, *John Sherman and Dhoya* achieved a good degree of success. The reviews, as Yeats commented, were "nearly all good."[21] To cite just one example, an unidentified critic in the *Westminster Review* for February, 1892, made the following comment:

> The first story, *John Sherman*, is not at all like the ordinary run of fiction, either in its incidents or its characters, and maintains throughout a pleasant subdued interest. *Dhoya* is a wild imaginative legend of a fiercely raging Irish giant. . . . His story is very skilfully told; the treatment and the accessories are large and heroic; there is none of that *mièvrerie* which often mars such attempts, jarring, in its modern sentimentalism, like a false note.[22]

Reviews like this enabled Unwin to issue two more printings of *John Sherman and Dhoya*, one in 1891 and the other in 1892; in addition, the book had been almost simultaneously published in America in 1891. Yeats, who was to receive a royalty only if the work reached "its second thousand if it ever does so," excitedly wrote to John

O'Leary that he stood to gain £30, "which will be very good indeed for a first story."[23]

In later years, however, Yeats came to have doubts about the artistic value of *John Sherman and Dhoya*. His 1904 judgment of the work is found in an inscription in Paul Lemperly's copy: "Written when I was very young & knew no better."[24] Three years later, when he was preparing the texts for the eight-volume *Collected Works in Verse & Prose*, Yeats was even hesitant about including the stories in his canon. He wrote to A. H. Bullen, the publisher of the collected edition, in July of 1907 about the contents of the unfinished volumes:

> C. *The Secret Rose, John Sherman, Dhoya*. (Very careful verbal revision necessary and two new stories desirable.)[25]

Yeats was far too pressed with work, however, to write two new stories. *John Sherman and Dhoya*, therefore, did appear in the seventh volume of the *Collected Works*, Yeats noting in an added preface that he had included the stories "somewhat against my judgment." In later years this judgment obviously took precedence: neither *John Sherman* nor *Dhoya* was included in the 1925 *Early Poems and Stories* or the posthumously published *Mythologies* of 1959.[26] The 1908 edition thus marks the last time that the stories were reprinted by Yeats.

*Dhoya*

In an article entitled "Ireland's Heroic Age," printed in *The Boston Pilot* for May 17, 1890, Yeats put forth the following proposition:

> The first thing needful if an Irish literature more elaborate and intense than our fine but primitive ballads is to come into being is that readers and writers alike should really know the imaginative periods of Irish history.[27]

As we have noted, almost three years earlier he had written *Dhoya*; and by so doing, he had concerned himself with just such an imaginative period of Irish history, in this instance one of the most remote of all.

*Dhoya* takes place in what Yeats called "those mysterious pre-human ages when life lasted for hundreds of years"[28] —the era of Irish "history" dealt with in what is now called by scholars the Mythological Cycle. This setting is established by the reference to Dhoya once being a captive of the Fomorians.

The exact identity of the Fomorians is a somewhat ambiguous issue in Irish mythology. Nicholas O'Kearney, whose *Feis Tigh Chonain* is referred to by Yeats in "Ganconagh's Apology," considered the Fomorians to be followers of Partholan, supposedly the conqueror of Ireland some three hundred years after the Deluge. According to O'Kearney, "it is quite clear that Partholanus and his people were Fomorians, who . . . were a branch of the tribes that originally held possession of the Promised Land, and who spread themselves from the African coasts."[29]

O'Kearney's opinion, however, is not the standard one given by most Irish writers; more usually, the Fomorians are pictured as distinct from Partholan and his followers. In Keating's *History of Ireland*, to cite just one example, the Fomorians are said to have been living in Ireland for some two hundred years before they are defeated by Partholan at the Battle of Mag Itha.[30] A few hundred years later, the Fomorians reappear on the scene as the oppressors of the Nemedians, the second conquerors of Ireland after the Deluge. At this point in the *History of Ireland*, Keating relates the accepted genealogy of the Fomorians: they are African pirates descended from the race of Ham and fleeing the curse of Noah.[31] Eventually, according to Keating, the Fomorians were vanquished by the Tuatha De Danaans at the Battle of North Moytura (in county Sligo, by the way).[32]

In treating the Fomorians as an historical race, however, both O'Kearney and Keating have ignored their mythologi-

13

cal origin as evil deities. As Douglas Hyde pointed out in *The Story of Early Gaelic Literature* (1894), the transformation of Irish gods into human beings was primarily the result of two factors:

> first from the rationalizing or euhemerizing tendencies of the early Irish, and secondly from the desire of the mediaevalists to trace back the history and kings of Ireland to Adam, after the fashion of the Hebrew pedigrees with which the introduction of Christianity made them acquainted.[33]

In particular, as Hyde later maintained in *A Literary History of Ireland* (1899), the standard derivation of "Fomor" as "along the seas," given by Keating and accepted by later commentators, was mistaken: the correct etymology "seems to point to a mythological origin 'men from under sea.' "[34]

Now as we know from the many notes ascribed to Douglas Hyde in *Fairy and Folk Tales of the Irish Peasantry* (1888), Yeats was accustomed to consult with Hyde on any matter involving Gaelic writings. It is not surprising, then, that Yeats should be aware of both the mortal and the mythological nature of the Fomorians. Clearly, in *Dhoya* they are basically presented as African sea-robbers, a treatment in accord with Yeats's reference in an 1889 newspaper article to the ages "when the monstrous race of the Fomorians, with one foot, and one arm in the middle of their chests, rushed in their pirate galleys century after century like clouds upon the coast."[35] At the same time, though, Dhoya's allusion to "Partholan, whose years were five hundred, sullen and solitary, sleeping only on the floor of the sea" would seem to indicate an awareness by Yeats of the mythological nature of the Fomorians—and perhaps also of O'Kearney's view of Partholan as a Fomorian leader. And indeed, the note on "Fomoroh" in *The Wanderings of Oisin*, likewise published in 1889, concentrates on the mythological level:

> Fomoroh means from under the sea, and is the name of the gods of night and death and cold. The Fomoroh were misshapen and had now the heads of goats and bulls, and now

but one leg, and one arm that came out of the middle of their breasts. They were the ancestors of the evil faeries and, according to one Gaelic writer, of all misshapen persons. The giants and the leprecauns are expressly mentioned as of the Fomoroh.[36]

Yeats is, of course, writing imaginative fiction and not mythological history; therefore, the exact identity of the Fomorians is not a crucial issue in *Dhoya*. Rather, Yeats has chosen the setting of the tale for two basic reasons. On the one hand, the age in which the story takes place obviously allowed the young and inexperienced writer total imaginative freedom in such matters as character and plot. More importantly, Yeats at this period of his career was wholly committed to an art which would be peculiarly Irish; the use of Irish mythology was one method by which this goal could easily be attained. As he wrote in a newspaper article in November, 1892:

Our history is full of incidents well worthy of drama, story and song. And they are incidents involving types of character of which this world has not yet heard. If we can put those tumultuous centuries into tale or drama, the whole world will listen to us and sit at our feet like children who hear a new story.[37]

Yeats was especially attracted to Irish mythology and folklore because he believed them to be a living tradition, part and parcel of the daily life of the Irishman—particularly of the peasant. As late as 1937 he stated that Irish mythology and legends "differ from those of other European countries because down to the end of the seventeenth century they had the attention, perhaps the unquestioned belief, of peasant and noble alike; . . . even to-day our ancient queens, our mediaeval soldiers and lovers, can make a pedlar shudder."[38] In fact, the existence of an actual "Pool Dhoya" in Sligo Bay (the deepest part, Mrs. Sheelah Kirby tells me[39]) makes it quite likely that *Dhoya* is, in the manner of many of *The Celtic Twilight* (1893) stories, Yeats's reworking of a local legend. The reference at the end of the story to "the cotters on the mountains of Donegal" who still say "there goes Dhoya" attempts to establish exactly such an oral tradition behind the tale.

Another way in which *Dhoya* reflects Yeats's belief in a living folk tradition is through the allusions to the Diarmuid and Grainne story. Rather than following the standard redaction of the legend—Standish Hayes O'Grady's "Pursuit after Diarmuid and Grainne," published in the *Transactions of the Ossianic Society for 1855*—Yeats has relied on the local Sligo traditions, gleaned from both the first volume of W. G. Wood-Martin's *History of Sligo* (1882) and conversations with local residents. Indeed, a letter written while he was still at work on *Dhoya* establishes the basis for Yeats's preference of the local traditions. Describing a trip "up Benbulben to see the place where Dermot died," he told Katharine Tynan that

> all peasants at the foot of the mountain know the legend, and know that Dermot still haunts the pool, and fear it. Every hill and stream is someway or other connected with the story.[40]

Thus, in *Dhoya* the meeting between the two lovers and Muadhan, who became their servant and "caught fish for them on a hook baited with a quicken-berry," is transferred from the Killarney area, where it takes place in O'Grady's version, to the plains around Sligo. Likewise, Yeats's allusion to the place where "Diarmuid hid in a deep cavern his Grania" clearly refers to the so-called "Diarmuid and Grania's bed," which Wood-Martin describes as "a natural cavern in the limestone-rock."[41] Finally, the mention of the island structure which Diarmuid constructed to hide Grania alludes to a *crannoge*, or "wooden structure," discussed at some length in the *History of Sligo*. As Wood-Martin noted, "two crannoges rested on Glencar Lake in olden times. . . . The smaller crannoge is supposed to have been a 'fishing lodge' of the renowned Dermod."[42]

Moreover, the basic plot situation of *Dhoya*, consisting of a liaison between a mortal, Dhoya, and an unnamed fairy woman, is based on a common motif of Irish literature. As

Yeats remarked in a note to *The Wind Among the Reeds* (1899), "the old Gaelic literature is full of appeals of the goddess Danu to mortals whom they would bring into their country."[43] One example of this motif which Yeats surely knew was "Connla of the Golden Hair and the Fairy Maiden," printed in P. W. Joyce's *Old Celtic Romances* (1879)—a book which in 1895 Yeats placed on a list of the thirty most valuable Irish works.[44] The fairy woman's description in that story of *Tir-na-n-Og*, the Country of the Young, is similar to the one found in *Dhoya*:

> I have come from the Land of the Living—a land where there is neither old age, nor any breach of law. . . . We pass our time very pleasantly in feasting and harmless amusements, never growing old; and we have no quarrels or contentions.[45]

Yeats himself, of course, often used the interaction between mortals and fairies as the basis of his own works: "The Stolen Child," "The Wanderings of Oisin," "The Host of the Air," and *The Land of Heart's Desire* are only some of the well-known examples. Less familiar perhaps, but more to our purposes, is a story first published as "The Devil's Book" in *The National Observer* for November 26, 1892, and later included in *The Secret Rose* (1897) as "The Book of the Great Dhoul and Hanrahan the Red." As in *Dhoya*, the fairy is attracted to the mortal precisely because the mortal lacks the immutable and unvaried characteristics of the Sidhe. The mortal, in short, is subject to Change, the one quality lacking in *Tir-na-n-Og*. As Cleena of the Wave says to Hanrahan,

> I have loved you from the night I saw you lying on the Gray Rath, and saw you turning from side to side, for the fire in your heart would not let you rest. I love you, for you are fierce and passionate, and good and bad and not dim and wave-like as are the people of the Shee.[46]

Once we realize that Yeats is working within a common Irish folklore tradition, a number of the minor details in *Dhoya* become clearer. The fairy woman, for example,

17

should be seen as a type of the *Leanhaun Shee,* or "fairy mistress." As Yeats described this particular creature in *Fairy and Folk Tales of the Irish Peasantry,*

> she seeks the love of mortals. If they refuse, she must be their slave; if they consent, they are hers, and can only escape by finding another to take their place. The fairy lives on their life, and they waste away. Death is no escape from her. She is the Gaelic muse, for she gives inspiration to those she persecutes. The Gaelic poets die young, for she is restless, and will not let them remain long on earth—this malignant phantom.[47]

Although not all of the above description is applicable to the fairy in *Dhoya,* the connection of the *Leanhaun Shee* with the muse doubtless explains the presence of a poem in the story. In another use of Irish folklore, the male fairy with whom Dhoya battles is "red-capped" because "red is the colour of magic in every country, and has been so from the very earliest times. The caps of faeries and magicians are well-nigh always red."[48] Finally, the game of chess which Dhoya and the male fairy engage in is likewise a traditional element. Chess, as Standish Hayes O'Grady explained in the "Pursuit after Diarmuid and Grainne," "was the favorite game of the Irish in the most ancient times of which we have any account, as appears from the constant mention of it in almost all romantic tales."[49]

Although Yeats has thus drawn heavily on common elements in Irish folklore and mythology, it is important to note the major deviation from the tradition in *Dhoya.* Commonly, both in Irish folklore and in most of Yeats's works, the liaison between a mortal and a fairy, when successful, results in the mortal being carried away to *Tir-na-n-Og.* In *Dhoya,* however, the entire encounter remains centered in the physical world. As we shall see shortly, this change is of some importance.

From the preceding discussion alone, it might be possible to dismiss *Dhoya,* as Ernest A. Boyd did, as a "slight folk-tale *pastiche.*"[50] Likewise, the temptation exists to consider *Dhoya* an example of "apprentice work," inferior to the later stories of *The Celtic Twilight* and *The Secret Rose*. Although I think that this second point might be argued, it will perhaps be more profitable to show that both judgments err in not recognizing the importance of *Dhoya* in Yeats's career.

Although Yeats had published some short prose fiction as early as 1889, little critical attention had been given to those productions. The success with which *Dhoya* was greeted clearly encouraged Yeats to continue working in the genre of the short story. Particularly responsible for this encouragement was W. E. Henley, the editor of *The National Observer*. Yeats wrote Katharine Tynan in 1891 that Henley, who preferred *Dhoya* to *John Sherman*,[51] "has asked me for things like 'Dhoya' for the *National Observer*."[52] Since he believed that "a success with stories would solve many problems for me and I write them easily,"[53] Yeats was glad to meet Henley's request. Eventually, the stories which he submitted to *The National Observer* and other journals after 1891 were combined with the earlier tales to form such collections as *The Celtic Twilight* and *The Secret Rose*. In this respect, then, *Dhoya* is to some extent responsible for much of Yeats's prose fiction.

Although to a lesser extent than *John Sherman*, *Dhoya* can also be read as a partially autobiographical document. T. R. Henn, for instance, has observed that Dhoya, along with Oisin, is "an early dream-image of Yeats, just as Cuchulain is the last."[54] Dhoya, Oisin, and Cuchulain are all, of course, types of the active, passionate man to which Yeats had a lasting attraction. Doubtless all three were in his mind when he wrote "Under Ben Bulben":

> Swear by those horsemen, by those women
> Complexion and form prove superhuman,
> That pale, long-visaged company
> That air in immortality
> Completeness of their passion won;
> Now they ride the wintry dawn
> Where Ben Bulben sets the scene.[55]

Other autobiographical elements in *Dhoya* have been cogently noted by Richard Ellmann: "The story has many suggestions of psychological difficulties, including self-distrust, sexual fears, and a desire to burrow away from the world."[56]

Most importantly, it should be clear that *Dhoya* is an early projection of ideas which Yeats continued to employ in his later works. F. A. C. Wilson, for example, has discussed the parallels between *Dhoya* and *At the Hawk's Well* (1917): "The story seems beyond doubt to have had a shaping influence on the later dance-play; fire-ritual and solitary contemplation, lake or well, the descent of a goddess, vain pursuit and sexual loss, came to be concepts associated in Yeats's mind."[57] Although this point is well-taken, I think Wilson would agree that *Dhoya* had a more important influence on Yeats's work than simply a parallel with a particular later play.

Considered in its largest terms, *Dhoya* presents a contrast between two modes of existence: on the one hand, immutability and sterility, as represented by the lives of both Dhoya and the fairy maiden before their liaison; on the other hand, mutability and passion, as represented by their life together. We now understand why Yeats has varied from the general fairy-mortal liaison motif and placed the relationship in the mortal world. Passion and Change are necessarily concomitant qualities: "Only the changing, and moody, and angry, and weary can love," as the fairy woman explains.

Although *Dhoya* concludes with the death of the title character, the story nevertheless clearly celebrates the type of existence which, while subject to Change, still allows the presence of passion. Needless to say, the choice was not always so definite in Yeats's mind. The tension between the two modes of existence shadowed forth in *Dhoya* was to become an important theme in his later work, receiving its most complex and extended treatment, perhaps, in the two Byzantium poems.

"All races," Yeats wrote in 1922, "had their first unity

from a mythology that marries them to rock and hill."[58] In sum, *Dhoya*, while illustrating and, in one sense, contributing to that mythology, also presents strong arguments for the continuity and integrity of Yeats's career.

## John Sherman

In his introduction to *Representative Irish Tales*, a two-volume collection of Irish writers published in the same year as *John Sherman and Dhoya*, Yeats made the following remark:

> Irish literature is, and will be, however, the same in one thing for many a long day—in its nationality, its resolve to celebrate in verse and prose all within the four seas of Ireland. And why should it be otherwise? A man need not go further than his own hill-side or his own village to find every kind of passion and virtue. As Paracelsus wrote, "If thou tastest a crust of bread, thou tastest all the stars and all the heavens."[59]

Clearly, one of the main intentions of *John Sherman* is just such a celebration of Ireland, developed in the novelette through the contrast between "Ballah" and London. Indeed, Yeats once told John O'Leary that "the motif" of *John Sherman* "is hatred of London."[60]

Perhaps in a mild attempt to preserve the anonymity of the 1891 publication, Yeats called the Irish town in both *John Sherman* and *Dhoya* by the name of "Ballah." Even though he admitted in the preface added to the 1908 edition that "Sligo . . . is Ballah"—and replaced in that printing the fictional "Inniscrewin"[61] with the actual Innisfree —Yeats did not alter the name of the town in the text.

There are, I suggest, two reasons for this retention of "Ballah." On the one hand, "Ballah" is simply a more typical Irish placename than Sligo. Two of the towns not far from Sligo, for instance, are called Balla and Ballina. In ad-

21

dition, *ballagh*, *ballah*, and *bally*, meaning respectively "way," "fordmouth," and "town," are frequent elements in the names of Irish towns and villages.

More importantly, Yeats may have intended "Ballah" to produce overtones of Blake's "Beulah." As we know from "The Trembling of the Veil" (1926), Yeats had been introduced to Blake by his father at the age of "fifteen or sixteen."[62] Also, in the spring of 1889 Yeats began his collaboration with Edwin Ellis on the three-volume *Works of William Blake*.[63] As finally published in 1893, this edition describes "Beulah" as follows:

> Beulah, or the zenith, corresponds to the eyes, because in the symbolic zenith is the first beginning of eternal life, and in the eyes is the first union of subject and object, thought and nature, spirit and matter. Beulah—Bunyan's place of pleasant rest—is interpreted in the Concordance to mean "marriage." In Blake, it is a place of repose, ante-chamber of Inspiration, and dwelling of the muses, not like those of the Greeks.[64]

Thematically, this picture of "Beulah" is in accord with the treatment of "Ballah" in *John Sherman*. And the fact that Blake is directly referred to in the story would seem to reinforce the connection.

At any rate, throughout *John Sherman* "Ballah" is constantly praised and London constantly attacked. This position on the town-city dichotomy was also expressed by Yeats in a number of articles and stories written around the same time as *John Sherman*. Indeed, in a few instances we find a rather close similarity between an earlier article or story and *John Sherman*. For example, Sherman's attack on the "minorities" prevalent in cities, presented in the very opening section of the novelette, is almost identical to the beginning of "Village Ghosts," first printed in *The Scots Observer* for May 11, 1889 and included in the 1893 edition of *The Celtic Twilight: Men and Women, Dhouls and Faeries*:

> In the great cities we see so little of the world, we drift into our minority. In the little towns and villages there are no minorities; people are not numerous enough. You must see

the world there, perforce. Every man is himself a class; every hour carries its new challenge.[65]

Likewise, Sherman's other major criticism of the city—the inability of city residents to feel a "sense of possession"—was expressed by Yeats in an article on William Allingham published in the *Providence Sunday Journal* for September 2, 1888. Again, we find the same phrasing as in *John Sherman*:

> Perhaps, also, to fully understand these poems one needs to have been born and bred in one of the western Irish towns; to remember how it was the centre of your world, how the mountains and the river and the woods became a portion of your life forever; to have loved with a sense of possession even the roadside bushes where the roadside cotters hung their clothes to dry. That sense of possession was the very centre of the matter. Elsewhere you are only a passer-by, for everything is owned by so many that it is owned by no one.[66]

The particular city attacked in *John Sherman* is, of course, London, and hatred of London is a topic which permeates Yeats's letters of 1887–1891—especially those to Katharine Tynan. At various times, Yeats pictured London as "dull and dirty," "hateful," "horrid," "melancholy," "a desert"—the list could easily be expanded.[67] In the same way that Sherman considered London "a reef whereon he was cast away," Yeats once told Miss Tynan that he felt "like Robinson Crusoe in this dreadful London."[68] A letter of 1888 which also mentions *John Sherman* provides a convenient summary of Yeats's attitude toward the English capital:

> There are still a hundred pages of Aesop—when they are done I shall get back to my story, in which I pour out all my grievances against this melancholy London—I sometimes imagine that the souls of the lost are compelled to walk through its streets perpetually. One feels them passing like a whiff of air.[69]

In addition to *John Sherman*, a little-known poem called "Street Dancers," first published in *The Wanderings of*

*Oisin,* is another instance in which this dislike of London found artistic expression:

> London streets have heritage,
> Blinder sorrows, harder wage—
> Sordid sorrows of the mart,
> Sorrows sapping brain and heart.[70]

From one point of view, this attack on urban life and the attendant praise of a more rural life is clearly a veneration of the pastoral ideal—certainly not an unusual theme to encounter in the Yeats of this period. However, we must also remember that *John Sherman* contrasts an English city with an Irish town: what is involved here is an exaltation not only of the pastoral but also of nationality in literature.

This question of a national basis for literature was, like the problems of city life, a topic much discussed by Yeats in his critical writings of the late eighties and early nineties. Indeed, for the sake of the argument Yeats often exaggerated his case, as in this statement from an 1891 newspaper article: "With Irish literature and Irish thought alone I have to do."[71] Polemics aside, though, Yeats was firmly committed to his beliefs that "cosmopolitan literature is, at best, but a poor bubble, though a big one" and that "creative work always has a fatherland."[72] The relationship between literature and nationality was, Yeats thought, a reciprocal one in which each element functioned to reinforce the other: literature gave unity to the nation, nationality gave depth to the literature. As he wrote in an article on Robert Browning, "there is no great literature without nationality, no great nationality without literature."[73] Thus, he informed Katharine Tynan in 1887 that "by being [as] Irish as you can, you will be more original and true to yourself and in the long run more interesting, even to English readers."[74]

As we have already seen, Yeats put this belief in the nationality of literature into artistic form by the use of Irish mythology in *Dhoya.* The praise of Irish life in *John Sherman* is likewise intended to accomplish the same aim.

24

Writing to Miss Tynan about a possible review of the novelette, Yeats insisted that the work be considered an "Irish novel":

> When you review it you might perhaps, if you think it is so, say that Sherman is an Irish type. I have an ambition to be taken as an Irish novelist, not as an English or cosmopolitan one choosing Ireland as a background. I studied my characters in Ireland and described a typical Irish feeling in Sherman's devotion to Ballah. . . . I claim for this and other reasons that *Sherman* is as much an Irish novel as anything by Banim or Griffin.[75]

The closeness of these two attitudes—the praise of Irish life and of nationality in literature—to Yeats's personal beliefs raises the question of autobiographical elements in *John Sherman*. Indeed, one does not have far to look: to a much greater extent than *Dhoya*, the novelette is based directly on Yeats's personal experiences. As he told Katharine Tynan in 1891, "there is more of myself in it than anything I have ever done."[76] Leaving aside for a moment John Sherman himself, it is clear that a number of the other personages in the story are sketches of actual people.

The character of Mrs. Sherman, for one example, is not far removed from that of Mrs. Susan Yeats, Yeats's mother. Mrs. Sherman's devotion to "Ballah" is parallel to Mrs. Yeats's attitude towards Sligo: as Yeats noted in *Estrangement* (1926), his mother "loved Sligo where she was born and bred with the same passion" that he himself did.[77] In a like manner, Sherman's uncle, Michael Sherman, is at least partially based on Yeats's grandfather, William Pollexfen —the co-director, along with William Middleton, of a steamship company. (The death of Middleton, like that of Saunders in the story, eventually left the control of the firm in the hands of Pollexfen.) One of the ways in which Michael Sherman and William Pollexfen are connected is their reticence. Sherman characterizes his uncle as a man "who never speaks"; in "Reveries Over Childhood and Youth" (1926), Yeats calls his grandfather "solitary and silent."[78]

This autobiographical level of *John Sherman* extends to even the most minor characters. The "very dirty old woman sitting by a crate of geese" on the steamer to Liverpool, for instance, is based on Yeats's remembrance of a childhood encounter. Describing in "Reveries Over Childhood and Youth" his arrival at the Liverpool dock to board one of his grandfather's ships for the journey to Ireland, Yeats narrates the following incident:

> When I was a little boy, an old woman who had come to Liverpool with crates of fowl made me miserable by throwing her arms around me, the moment I had alighted from my cab, and telling the sailor who carried my luggage that she had held me in her arms when I was a baby.[79]

A more interesting, but also more speculative, autobiographical element in *John Sherman* concerns the identity of the heroine, Mary Carton. The name "Mary Carton" would seem to indicate a connection with Mary Cronan, the girl to whom the earliest extant letter of Yeats, written probably not later than 1884, is addressed.[80] Since at the present time there is no information available about Mary Cronan, this connection must remain open to question: it is possible that the similarity between the two women is a matter of names only (though I doubt it).

One statement about the women in *John Sherman* can be more definitely made: neither Mary Carton nor Margaret Leland is based to any significant degree on Maud Gonne. It was not until January 30, 1889 that the fateful meeting with Miss Gonne took place;[81] by that time, as noted earlier, *John Sherman* was basically completed. However, Maud Gonne is not totally unconnected with the novelette. In 1891 Yeats apparently considered dedicating *John Sherman and Dhoya* to her: two of the poems in the vellum manuscript book which he presented to Miss Gonne are written under the heading of "Dedication of 'John Sherman and Dhoya.'"[82]

The question of Yeats's source for the character of John Sherman presents a more complex problem. On the one hand, Sherman is, as both Joseph Hone and Norman Jeffares agree, partially based on Henry Middleton, a cousin of Yeats and one of his childhood playmates.[83] Secondly, we have already observed that there is a great deal of Yeats himself in John Sherman. In addition to the similarities of their opinions on London and Sligo, Sherman's desire to escape from the difficulties of life by retreating to Innisfree is clearly a deeply personal element. The letter to Katharine Tynan on December 21, 1888, which contains the first version of "The Lake Isle of Innisfree," stresses this connection: "In my story I make one of the characters whenever he is in trouble long to go away and live alone on that Island—an old daydream of my own."[84]

John Sherman is not, however, simply Yeats's autobiographical sketch of himself. Rather, Sherman and the Reverend William Howard together present an early illustration of that division of personality which Yeats was later to treat by means of such terms as the Self and the Anti-Self. That is, both characters represent segments of what was, at least for Yeats, an unattainable total or complete personality. Therefore, as Richard Ellmann has perceptively noted, "Yeats is both characters."[85]

The basic division between the two characters is brought into focus by Howard's remark in the fourth part of the novelette:

> . . . you Shermans are a deep people, much deeper than we Howards. We are like moths or butterflies, or rather rapid rivulets, while you and yours are deep pools in the forest where the beasts go to drink. No! I have a better metaphor. Your mind and mine are two arrows. Yours has got no feathers, and mine has no metal on the point.

In the largest terms of this division it is clear that Sherman represents the Self, Howard the Anti-Self: Sherman is subjective, Howard objective; Sherman is introverted, Howard extroverted; Sherman is the man of the country, a Romanticist; Howard the man of the city, a Classicist. In brief, Sherman is what the Yeats of the late 1880's was; Howard is what he considered trying to become.

27

The opposite nature of Sherman and Howard is illustrated in a number of contrasting details. Howard's handwriting, for example, is described as "small and beautiful"; Sherman, on the other hand, was "a laborious and unpractised writer, and found it helped him to make a pencil copy." Howard is extremely concerned about his appearance: he "did not even feel upright and clever when his hat was getting old." Sherman, by way of contrast, "grew shabbier and shabbier, and at the same time more and more cheerful." Even their chess tactics are diametrically opposed. When Howard finds Sherman one night playing chess against himself (along with the hedge which divides Sherman's garden in two, another indication of the division of personality in the story), he suggests that they play a game together:

> Sherman relied most upon his bishops and his queen. Howard was fondest of the knights. At first Sherman was the attacking party, but in his characteristic desire to scheme out his game many moves ahead, kept making slips, and at last had to give up, with his men nearly all gone and his king hopelessly cornered.

A fourth detail which separates the two characters is their religious beliefs. Sherman, as Margaret tells him, is more or less orthodox. Howard, even though he is a High Church curate, holds some rather heterodox opinions: he loses his parish through preaching a sermon to prove that children who die unbaptized are lost. Moreover, in a manner quite reminiscent of Florian Deleal in Pater's "The Child in the House" (1878), Howard "delighted in the intricacies of High Church costume" and "put candles on the altar and crosses in unexpected places."

To turn to some larger issues, we must note the contrast between the poetical nature of Sherman and the unpoetical nature of Howard. Howard, in fact, is specifically criticized by the narrator for his lack of a poetic sensibility:

> . . . his efficiency gave to all his thoughts a certain over-completeness and isolation, and a kind of hardness to his mind. His intellect was like a musician's instrument with no

sounding-board. He could think carefully and cleverly and even with originality, but never in such a way as to make his thoughts an allusion to something deeper than themselves. In this he was the reverse of poetical, for poetry is essentially a touch from behind a curtain.

In direct antithesis to this rather sterile intellectualism of Howard, Sherman's mind was "clucking continually over its brood of thoughts": that is, finding in the common objects around him continual allusions to things "deeper than themselves." This poetic construct of Sherman's mind is exemplified in an extended passage which eventually terminates in the well-known description of Innisfree:

> Delayed by a crush in the Strand, he heard a faint trickling of water near by; it came from a shop window where a little water-jet balanced a wooden ball upon its point. The sound suggested a cataract with a long Gaelic name, that leaped crying into the Gate of the Winds at Ballah. Wandering among these memories a footstep went to and fro continually, and the figure of Mary Carton moved among them like a phantom.

This particular section of *John Sherman* ends with a sentence which effectively summarizes and reinforces this basic contrast between the two characters: "The light that dazzled him [Sherman] flowed from the vague and refracting regions of hope and memory;[86] the light that made Howard's feet unsteady was ever the too-glaring lustre of life itself."

Another central issue on which Sherman and Howard hold opposite views is the dichotomy between "Ballah" and London. As we have seen, Sherman continually attacks London and yearns "to see again the town where he had spent his childhood." Howard, on the other hand, considers "Ballah" simply "intolerable": "Here everybody lives in the eighteenth century—the squalid century. Well, I am going to-morrow, you know. Thank Heaven, I am done with your grey streets and grey minds!"

This contrast between the two characters is reinforced by the picture which each of them draws of his ideal mode of life. Howard, naturally enough, sees himself in relation to a city:

> I also have planned my future. Not too near or too far from a great city I see myself in a cottage with diamond panes, sitting by the fire. There are books everywhere and etchings on the wall. On the table is a manuscript essay on some religious matter.

Sherman, though, desires a more pastoral existence: "I should have a house in the country; I should hunt and shoot, and have a garden and three gardeners." Later, after he has decided to marry Mary Carton, Sherman moderates these goals, making them even more idyllic: "a small house with a green door and a new thatch, and a row of beehives under a hedge."

But the antithesis seen in these contrasting pictures is between not only cosmopolitan and pastoral life but also Classicism and Romanticism. Howard desires a life which is intellectualized, controlled, and static; Sherman desires a life which is unintellectualized, loosely controlled, and active. Moreover, the libraries of the two characters reinforce this distinction. Howard's collection is an eclectic one, "in which Cardinal Newman and Bourget,[87] St. Chrysostom and Flaubert lived together in perfect friendship." Sherman's library contains "a Shakespeare," "a few two-shilling novels," "a volume on etiquette," and two works typical of Romanticism: Percy's *Reliques of Ancient English Poetry*, the most important collection of English ballads, and Mungo Park's *Travels into the Interior Districts of Africa*, an illustrative example of Romantic travel literature.

Although many other antitheses between Sherman and Howard could be cited, it should be clear that the differences which we have noted make inevitable Sherman's final rejection of Margaret Leland and his marriage with Mary Carton. Margaret's opinions on society, on dress, on the "miserable little town" of Ballah "with its sleepy old shops and its sleepy old society" are all basically identical with those of Howard and need not be discussed in detail. As

Sherman himself summarizes, "Margaret glitters and glitters, but she is not of my kind." His marriage with Mary Carton is thus an affirmation of his own beliefs.

The details of *John Sherman*, then, all lend support to the view that John Sherman and the Reverend William Howard are clearly antithetical characters: as Sherman comments, "their strong friendship was founded in a great measure on mutual contempt." Although it is clear that Yeats's own sympathy at this time of his life was with John Sherman, we must remember that this opinion is never extended to the point of, say, ridiculing Howard. We should also note that Yeats himself was well aware of the basic division in the novel and of the inherent artistic danger of thereby creating type characters—a potential fault which I think Yeats has avoided. As he wrote to John O'Leary in 1888,

> my novel or novelette draws to a close. . . . It is all about a curate and a young man from the country. The difficulty is to keep the characters from turning into eastern symbolic monsters of some sort, which would be a curious thing to happen to a curate and a young man from the country.[88]

And finally, it can also be seen that the novel as a whole is structured around contrasting pairs: the antithesis between Sherman and Howard is carried out between Mary Carton and Margaret Leland and between Mrs. Sherman and Mrs. Leland; the action of the novel is divided almost evenly between Sligo and London; and all the major scenes of the work involve only two characters.

*John Sherman*, then, must be seen as an early statement of a central Yeatsian concern. Although the terminology was to vary greatly—from Michael Robartes and Owen Aherne of *The Secret Rose* (1897), to the Self and the Anti-Self of *Per Amica Silentia Lunae* (1917), to the more complex constructs of *A Vision* (1926, 1937)—the sense of a divided self remained a consistent and important element of Yeats's thought.

*John Sherman* is also an interesting work in that its style and mood are unique among Yeats's published prose fiction. As he told Father Matthew Russell in 1891, "people are given to thinking I can write only of the fantastic and wild, and this book has to do, so far as the long story is concerned, with very ordinary persons and events."[89] Indeed, *John Sherman* well illustrates Yeats's belief that "real novel writing," as he told Lady Gregory in 1900, should primarily consist of "characterization and conversation."[90]

Any final evaluation of *John Sherman*, in sum, should recognize Yeats's intentions in writing the story. Such an analysis must also, I think, reject the rather fulsome praise of early critics like Ernest A. Boyd—"Had the Literary Revival produced a novelist, we should have expected him to make this book a point of departure"[91]—in favor of a more tempered judgment. Perhaps Yeats's own comment on *John Sherman* best expresses that kind of moderate evaluation:

> I don't imagine it will please many people but some few it may please with some kind of permanent pleasure. Except for the wish to make a little money, I have no desire to get that kind of fussing regard a book wins from the many. To please the folk of few books is one's great aim. By being Irish, I think, one has a better chance of it.[92]

*Textual Revisions*

There are three important textual variants between the 1891 English and American editions of *John Sherman and Dhoya*. All three occur at the beginning of sections of the novelette. In two instances (II, i; V, iii), the variants consist of simply a reversal in sentence structure. The other instance (III, ii) involves a change in both sentence structure and wording: "He arrived in the town of Ballah by rail" in the English printing becomes "The town of Ballah he reached by rail" in the American printing. In addition to these three major variants, there are other minor discrepancies between the two editions: in *Dhoya*, for example, the penultimate paragraph ends with "Western Sea" in the English edition and "Western Deep" in the American edition.

The reason for these and other variants between the two 1891 printings must remain open to question. The American and English editions were apparently published almost simultaneously. Although the English edition was not released until November, 1891, Yeats must have had review copies available by at least October of that year—as can be seen in Edward Dowden's use of a quotation from *John Sherman* in *The Fortnightly Review* for November 1, 1891.[93] The American edition of *John Sherman and Dhoya* was entered for copyright at the Library of Congress on October 2, 1891, and two copies were received there on November 10, 1891.[94]

On the one hand, then, this simultaneous publication may have necessitated the preparation by Yeats of two copies of the text; if so, it would not have been unlike his usual practice to have made some textual revisions while preparing the second copy. On the other hand, it is also possible that the variants between the two 1891 printings are simply the result of printer's errors. Considering the nature of the variants, though, I suggest that the first explanation is the more probable one.

We are on much firmer ground, however, in discussing the revisions made for the inclusion of *John Sherman and Dhoya* in the 1908 *Collected Works in Verse & Prose*. As both the two variorum editions and the work of several scholars has conclusively shown, Yeats almost never reprinted any of his work without subjecting it to a careful process of revision. Moreover, he was particularly insistent that the *Collected Works* represent his final wishes: he told A. H. Bullen in 1907 that "I will not have one word printed that I have not seen and passed. . . . This will be my final text for years, and I refuse to have any portion of that text settled by any person but myself."[95] We can thus be confident that the changes made for the 1908 printing are Yeats's own.

Considered in terms of his usual practice, the revisions made in *John Sherman and Dhoya* are fewer than might be expected. Nevertheless, they do show that Yeats went through the text with care. In *John Sherman*, for one example, Yeats eliminated the foreign words: "*recherché*" is changed to "distinguished" (I, i); with more regret, we notice that the Gaelic *gluggerabunthaun*, meaning more or less "empty-rattling-arse,"[96] is removed altogether (I, i).

Yeats also altered *John Sherman* by removing some descriptive phrases or words which tended to be exaggerative. Instead of the 1891 reference to "a clothes-moth in an antimacassar thought the end of the world had come and fluttered out," we find in 1908 only "a clothes-moth fluttered out" (II, ii). Likewise, after the 1891 printings Margaret no longer describes the *Imitation of Christ* as "sweet" (IV, v).

Finally, in a few places in *John Sherman* Yeats attempted to produce a tighter sentence structure by eliminating unnecessary words and altering the syntax. For example, he revised "I hold that when we have lost the directness and sincerity of our nature we have no compass" to "I hold the directness and sincerity of the nature to be its compass" (I, i).

The revisions made in *Dhoya* are of a quite similar nature to those already discussed. The change of "prayer to the moon before turning to sleep again—the moon that glimmered through the door of his cave," for instance, to "prayer to the moon that glimmered through the door of his cave before turning to sleep again" (I) results in a somewhat tighter sentence structure by eliminating the repetition of "moon." Likewise, the removal of "wildly" and "with a wild leap" (III) gives a less exaggerated tone to the conclusion of the story.

As can be seen from the textual notes, there are a great number of minor changes not cited here. Taken all together, though, the revisions made to *John Sherman and Dhoya* do not show any important modification in Yeats's conception of the two stories. Rather, the revisions illustrate the attention Yeats gave to the details of his work— including his prose fiction. As he wrote in 1908,

> The friends that have it I do wrong
> When ever I remake a song,
> Should know what issue is at stake:
> It is myself that I remake.[97]

## A Note on the Text

*John Sherman and Dhoya* has been previously published three times. These printings, preceded by the abbreviations used to refer to them in the textual notes, are as follows:

L:  Ganconagh. *John Sherman and Dhoya*. London: T. Fisher Unwin, 1891.
NY:  Ganconagh. *John Sherman and Dhoya*. New York: Cassell Publishing Company, 1891.
CW:  William Butler Yeats. *The Collected Works in Verse & Prose*. Volume VII. Stratford-on-Avon: The Shakespeare Head Press, 1908.

The text used as the basis of this edition is the one found in CW. As indicated in the textual notes, I have varied from CW in only three respects: the indentation of the opening paragraph of each story; and the change of the obviously incorrect "illusion" and "beside" of CW to the proper "allusion" of L and NY and "besides" of NY.

The textual notes, located at the foot of each page, present a complete collation of the three texts. The numbers preceding these notes on any page refer to the line numbers of the text on that page. I have attempted to give sufficient wording around each variant to provide clarity.

The only discrepancy among the three printings not cited in the textual notes concerns the headings of each of

Edward Miner Gallaudet Memorial Library

121830

the five sections of *John Sherman:* both *L* and NY have "Part I" instead of "First Part," and so on; also, *L* places the number and title of each section on a separate page.

Superscript numbers in the text indicate the editor's explanatory notes which are located at the back of the book. These notes do not duplicate material already presented in the Introduction.

# JOHN SHERMAN

# &

# DHOYA:

## TWO EARLY STORIES

# GANCONAGH'S APOLOGY*

The maker of these stories has been told that he must not bring them to you himself. He has asked me to pretend that I am the author. I am an old little Irish spirit, and I sit in the hedges and watch the world go by. I see the boys going to market driving donkeys with creels of turf, and the girls carrying baskets of apples. Sometimes I call to some pretty face, and we chat a little in the shadow, the apple basket before us, for, as my faithful historian O'Kearney[1] has put it in his now yellow manuscript, I care for nothing in the world but love and idleness. Will not you, too, sit down under the shade of the bushes while I read you the stories? The first I do not care for because it deals with dull persons and the world's affairs, but the second has to do with my own people. If my voice at whiles grows distant and dreamy when I talk of the world's affairs, remember that I have seen all from my hole in the hedge. I hear continually the songs of my own people who dance upon the hill-side, and am content. I have never carried apples or driven turf myself, or if I did it was only in a dream. Nor do my kind use any of man's belongings except the little black pipes which the farmers find now and then when they are turning the sods over with a plow.

GANCONAGH.

* Found only in NY and L. Texts identical.

# [Preface to the 1908 edition]*

Having been persuaded somewhat against my judgment to include these early stories, I have read them for the first time these many years. They have come to interest me very deeply; for I am something of an astrologer, and can see in them a young man—was I twenty-three? and we Irish ripen slowly—born when the Water-Carrier was on the horizon, at pains to overcome Saturn in Saturn's hour,² just as I can see in much that follows his struggle with the still all-too-unconquered Moon, and at last, as I think, the summons of the prouder Sun.³ Sligo, where I had lived as a child and spent some months or weeks of every year till long after, is Ballah, and Pool Dhoya is at the river mouth there, and he who gave me all of Sherman that was not born at the rising of the Water-Carrier has still the bronze upon his face, and is at this moment, it may be, in his walled garden, wondering, as he did twenty years ago, whether he will ever mend the broken glass of the conservatory, where I am not too young to recollect the vine-trees and grapes that did not ripen.⁴

W. B. YEATS.

*November 14th, 1907.*

* Found only in CW.

40

# JOHN SHERMAN

# JOHN SHERMAN LEAVES BALLAH

## I

In the west of Ireland, on the 9th of December, in the town of Ballah, in the Imperial Hotel there was a single guest, clerical and youthful. With the exception of a stray commercial traveller, who stopped once for a night, there had been nobody for a whole month but this guest, and now he was thinking of going away. The town, full enough in summer of trout and salmon fishers, slept all winter like the bears.

On the evening of the 9th of December, in the coffee-room of the Imperial Hotel, there was nobody but this guest. The guest was irritated. It had rained all day, and now that it was clearing up night had almost fallen. He had packed his portmanteau; his stockings, his clothes-brush, his razor, his dress shoes were each in their corner, and now he had nothing to do. He had tried the paper that was lying on the table. He did not agree with its politics.

The waiter was playing an accordion in a little room over the stairs. The guest's irritation increased, for the more

1. [No paragraph indentation in CW. This lack of indentation at the beginning of a story is characteristic of CW.]
13. L: . . . portmanteau:        14. NY: . . . shoes, were . . . . his . . . .

he thought about it the more he perceived that the accordion was badly played. There was a piano in the coffee-room; he sat down at it and played the tune correctly, as loudly as possible. The waiter took no notice. He did not know that he was being played for. He was wholly absorbed in his own playing, and besides he was old, obstinate, and deaf. The guest could stand it no longer. He rang for the waiter, and then, remembering that he did not need anything, went out before he came.

He went through Martin's Street and Peter's Lane, and turned down by the burnt house at the corner of the fish-market, picking his way towards the bridge. The town was dripping, but the rain was almost over. The large drops fell seldomer and seldomer into the puddles. It was the hour of ducks. Three or four had squeezed themselves under a gate, and were now splashing about in the gutter of the main street. There was scarcely anyone abroad. Once or twice a countryman went by in yellow gaiters covered with mud and looked at the guest. Once an old woman with a basket of clothes, recognizing the Protestant curate's *locum tenens*, made a low curtsey.

The clouds gradually drifted away, the twilight deepened and the stars came out. The guest, having bought some cigarettes, had spread his waterproof on the parapet of the bridge and was now leaning his elbows upon it, looking at the river and feeling at last quite tranquil. His meditations, he repeated, to himself, were plated with silver by the stars. The water slid noiselessly, and one or two of the larger stars made little roadways of fire into the darkness. The light from a distant casement made also its roadway. Once or twice a fish leaped. Along the banks were the vague shadows of houses, seeming like phantoms gathering to drink.

Yes; he felt now quite contented with the world. Amidst his enjoyment of the shadows and the river—

10. *L, NY*: . . . Street, and . . .     21. *NY*: . . . courtesy.
12. *NY*: . . . fish market, . . . .     22. *NY*: . . . deepened, and . . . .
17. *L*: . . . any one . . . .          27. *NY*: . . . repeated to . . . .

a veritable festival of silence—was mixed pleasantly the knowledge that, as he leant there with the light of a neighbouring gas-jet flickering faintly on his refined form and nervous face and glancing from the little medal of some Anglican order that hung upon his watch-guard, he must have seemed—if there had been any to witness—a being of a different kind to the inhabitants—at once rough and conventional—of this half-deserted town. Between these two feelings the unworldly and the worldly tossed a leaping wave of perfect enjoyment. How pleasantly conscious of his own identity it made him when he thought how he and not those whose birthright it was, felt most the beauty of these shadows and this river! For him who had read much, seen operas and plays, known religious experiences, and written verse to a waterfall in Switzerland, and not for those who dwelt upon its borders for their whole lives, did this river raise a tumult of images and wonders. What meaning it had for them he could not imagine. Some meaning surely it must have!

As he gazed out into the darkness, spinning a web of thoughts from himself to the river, from the river to himself, he saw, with a corner of his eye, a spot of red light moving in the air at the other end of the bridge. He turned towards it. It came closer and closer, there appearing behind it the while a man and a cigar. The man carried in one hand a mass of fishing-line covered with hooks, and in the other a tin porringer full of bait.

'Good evening, Howard.'

'Good evening,' answered the guest, taking his elbows off the parapet and looking in a preoccupied way at the man with the hooks. It was only gradually he remembered that he was in Ballah among the barbarians, for his mind had strayed from the last evening flies, making circles on

2. NY: . . . neighboring . . .
3. L: . . . gas-jet, flickering . . . .
9. NY: . . . feelings, the . . .
9. NY: . . . worldly, tossed . . . .

11. NY: . . . he, and . . .
13. L: . . . river?
13. L, NY: To him . . .
15. L, NY: . . . to those . . . .
24. NY: . . . toward . . . .
33. L, NY: . . . evening gnats, . . .

the water beneath, to the devil's song against 'the little spirits' in *Mefistofele*. Looking down at the stone parapet he considered a moment and then burst out—

'Sherman, how do you stand this place—you who have thoughts above mere eating and sleeping and are not always grinding at the stubble mill? Here everybody lives in the eighteenth century—the squalid century. Well, I am going to-morrow, you know. Thank Heaven, I am done with your grey streets and grey minds! The curate must come home, sick or well. I have a religious essay to write, and besides I should die. Think of that old fellow at the corner there, our most important parishioner. There are no more hairs on his head than thoughts in his skull. To merely look at him is to rob life of its dignity. Then there is nothing in the shops but school-books and Sunday-school prizes. Excellent, no doubt, for anyone who has not had to read as many as I have. Such a choir! such rain!'

'You need some occupation peculiar to the place,' said the other, baiting his hooks with worms out of the little porringer. 'I catch eels. You should set some night-lines too. You bait them with worms in this way, and put them among the weeds at the edge of the river. In the morning you find an eel or two, if you have good fortune, turning round and round and making the weeds sway. I shall catch a great many after this rain.'

'What a suggestion! Do you mean to stay here,' said Howard, 'till your mind rots like our most important parishioner's?'

'No, no! To be quite frank with you,' replied the other, 'I have some good looks and shall try to turn them to account by going away from here pretty soon and trying to persuade some girl with money to fall in love with me. I shall not be altogether a bad match, you see, because after she has made me a little prosperous my uncle will die and make me much more so. I wish to be able always to remain

2. *L, NY:* . . . in "Mefistofele."     16. *L:* . . . any one . . . .
3. *NY:* . . . burst out: . . .         21. *NY:* . . . in its way . . . .
9. *NY:* . . . gray streets and gray    30. *NY:* . . . looks, and . . . .
   minds!

a lounger. Yes, I shall marry money. My mother has set her heart on it, and I am not, you see, the kind of person who falls in love inconveniently. For the present—'

'You are vegetating,' interrupted the other.

'No, I am seeing the world. In your big towns a man finds his minority and knows nothing outside its border. He knows only the people like himself. But here one chats with the whole world in a day's walk, for every man one meets is a class. The knowledge I am picking up may be useful to me when I enter the great cities and their ignorance. But I have lines to set. Come with me. I would ask you home, but you and my mother, you know, do not get on well.'

'I could not live with anyone I did not believe in,' said Howard; 'you are so different from me. You can live with mere facts, and that is why, I suppose, your schemes are so mercenary. Before this beautiful river, these stars, these great purple shadows, do you not feel like an insect in a flower? As for me, I also have planned my future. Not too near or too far from a great city, I see myself in a cottage with diamond panes, sitting by the fire. There are books everywhere and etchings on the wall; on the table is a manuscript essay on some religious matter. Perhaps I shall marry some day. Probably not, for I shall ask so much. Certainly I shall not marry for money, for I hold that when we have lost the directness and sincerity of our nature we have no compass. If we once break it the world grows trackless.'

'Good-bye,' said Sherman, briskly; 'I have baited the last hook. Your schemes suit you, but a sluggish fellow like me, poor devil, who wishes to lounge through the world, would find them expensive.'

They parted; Sherman to set his lines and Howard to his hotel in high spirits, for it seemed to him he had been eloquent. The billiard-room, which opened on the street, was lighted up. A few young men came round to play sometimes. He went in, for among these provincial youths

13. L: . . . any one . . . .          directness and sincerity of the
19. L, NY: . . . city I . . . .        nature to be its compass.
24. L, NY: . . . for I hold the    28. NY: 'Good-by,' . . . .

he felt distinguished; besides, he was a really good player. As he came in one of the players missed and swore. Howard reproved him with a look. He joined the play for a time, and then catching sight through a distant door of the hotel-keeper's wife putting a kettle on the hob he hurried off, and, drawing a chair to the fire, began one of those long gossips about everybody's affairs peculiar to the cloth.

As Sherman, having set his lines, returned home, he passed a tobacconist's—a sweet-shop and tobacconist's in one—the only shop in town, except public-houses, that remained open. The tobacconist was standing in his door, and, recognizing one who dealt consistently with a rival at the other end of the town, muttered: 'There goes that Jack o' Dreams; been fishing most likely. Ugh!' Sherman paused for a moment as he repassed the bridge and looked at the water, on which now a new-risen and crescent moon was shining dimly. How full of memories it was to him! what playmates and boyish adventures did it not bring to mind! To him it seemed to say, 'Stay near to me,' as to Howard it had said, 'Go yonder, to those other joys and other sceneries I have told you of.' It bade him who loved stay still and dream, and gave flying feet to him who imagined.

## II

The house where Sherman and his mother lived was one of those bare houses so common in country towns. Their dashed fronts mounting above empty pavements have a kind of dignity in their utilitarianism. They seem to say, 'Fashion has not made us, nor ever do its caprices pass our sand-cleaned doorsteps.' On every basement window is the same dingy wire blind; on every door the same brass knocker. Custom everywhere! 'So much the longer,' the blinds seem to say, 'have eyes glanced through us'; and the knockers to murmur, 'And fingers lifted us.'

1. L, NY: . . . felt *recherché*;
 . . . .
9. NY: . . . tobacconist's,—. . .
9. NY: . . . in one,— . . . .
13. NY: . . . muttered, 'There . . .
13. L, NY: . . . that *gluggerabun-*

*thaun* and Jack . . . .
25. NY: . . . fronts, mounting above empty pavements, have . . . .

No. 15, Stephens' Row, was in no manner peculiar among its twenty fellows. The chairs in the drawing-room facing the street were of heavy mahogany with horsehair cushions worn at the corners. On the round table was somebody's commentary on the New Testament laid like the spokes of a wheel on a table-cover of American oilcloth with stamped Japanese figures half worn away. The room was seldom used, for Mrs. Sherman was solitary because silent. In this room the dressmaker sat twice a year, and here the rector's wife used every month or so to drink a cup of tea. It was quite clean. There was not a fly-mark on the mirror, and all summer the fern in the grate was constantly changed. Behind this room and overlooking the garden was the parlour, where cane-bottomed chairs took the place of mahogany. Sherman had lived here with his mother all his life, and their old servant hardly remembered having lived anywhere else; and soon she would absolutely cease to remember the world she knew before she saw the four walls of this house, for every day she forgot something fresh. The son was almost thirty, the mother fifty, and the servant near seventy. Every year they had two hundred pounds among them, and once a year the son got a new suit of clothes and went into the drawing-room to look at himself in the mirror.

On the morning of the 10th of December Mrs. Sherman was down before her son. A spare, delicate-featured woman, with somewhat thin lips tightly closed as with silent people, and eyes at once gentle and distrustful, tempering the hardness of the lips. She helped the servant to set the table, and then, for her old-fashioned ideas would not allow her to rest, began to knit, often interrupting her knitting to go into the kitchen or to listen at the foot of the stairs. At last, hearing a sound upstairs, she put the eggs down to boil, muttering the while, and began again to knit.

1. NY: No. 15 Stephen's Row was . . . .
4. NY: . . . cushions, worn . . . .
5. NY: . . . Testament, laid . . .
6. NY: . . . table cover . . . .
13. NY: . . . room, and overlooking the garden, was the parlor, . . . .
25. L, NY: . . . the 20th of . . . .
27. NY: . . . closed, as . . . .

When her son appeared she received him with a smile.

'Late again, mother,' he said.

'The young should sleep,' she answered, for to her he seemed still a boy.

She had finished her breakfast some time before the young man, and because it would have appeared very wrong to her to leave the table, she sat on knitting behind the tea-urn: an industry the benefit of which was felt by many poor children—almost the only neighbours she had a good word for.

'Mother,' said the young man, presently, 'your friend the *locum tenens* is off to-day.'

'A good riddance.'

'Why are you so hard on him? He talked intelligently when here, I thought,' answered her son.

'I do not like his theology,' she replied, 'nor his way of running about and flirting with this body and that body, nor his way of chattering while he buttons and unbuttons his gloves.'

'You forget he is a man of the great world, and has about him a manner that must seem strange to us.'

'Oh he might do very well,' she answered, 'for one of those Carton girls at the rectory.'

'That eldest girl is a good girl,' replied her son.

'She looks down on us all, and thinks herself intellectual,' she went on. 'I remember when girls were content with their catechism and their Bibles and a little practice at the piano, maybe, for an accomplishment. What does any one want more? It is all pride.'

'You used to like her as a child,' said the young man.

'I like all children.'

Sherman having finished his breakfast, took a book of travels in one hand and a trowel in the other and went out into the garden. Having looked under the parlour window

6. NY: . . . and, because . . .   17. NY: . . . body; nor . . . .
8. NY: . . . tea-urn; an . . .   27. L, NY: . . . Catechism . . . .
9. NY: . . . neighbors . . . .   32. NY: Sherman, having . . . .
11. NY: . . . man presently, . . .   34. NY: . . . parlor . . . .
12. L, NY: . . . off to-morrow.'

50

for the first tulip shoots, he went down to the further end and began covering some sea-kale for forcing. He had not been long at work when the servant brought him a letter. There was a stone roller at one side of the grass plot. He sat down upon it, and taking the letter between his finger and thumb began looking at it with an air that said: 'Well! I know what you mean.' He remained long thus without opening it, the book lying beside him on the roller.

The garden—the letter—the book! You have there the three symbols of his life. Every morning he worked in that garden among the sights and sounds of nature. Month by month he planted and hoed and dug there. In the middle he had set a hedge that divided the garden in two. Above the hedge were flowers; below it, vegetables. At the furthest end from the house, lapping broken masonry full of wall-flowers, the river said, month after month to all upon its banks, 'Hush!' He dined at two with perfect regularity, and in the afternoon went out to shoot or walk. At twilight he set night-lines. Later on he read. He had not many books —a Shakespeare, Mungo Park's travels, a few two-shilling novels, *Percy's Reliques*, and a volume on etiquette. He seldom varied his occupations. He had no profession. The town talked of it. They said: 'He lives upon his mother,' and were very angry. They never let him see this, however, for it was generally understood he would be a dangerous fellow to rouse; but there was an uncle from whom Sherman had expectations who sometimes wrote remonstrating. Mrs. Sherman resented these letters, for she was afraid of her son going away to seek his fortune—perhaps even in America. Now this matter preyed somewhat on Sherman. For three years or so he had been trying to make his mind up and come to some decision. Sometimes when reading he would start and press his lips together and knit his brows for a moment.

It will now be seen why the garden, the book, and the letter were the three symbols of his life, summing up as

12. NY: [new paragraph begins here.]
15. NY: . . . wallflowers; the . . . .
19. NY: . . . night lines.
21. L, NY: . . . novels, "Percey's Reliques," and . . . .

they did his love of out-of-door doings, his meditations, his anxieties. His life in the garden had granted serenity to his forehead, the reading of his few books had filled his eyes with reverie, and the feeling that he was not quite a good citizen had given a slight and occasional trembling to his lips.

He opened the letter. Its contents were what he had long expected. His uncle offered to take him into his office. He laid it spread out before him—a foot on each margin, right and left—and looked at it, turning the matter over and over in his mind. Would he go? would he stay? He did not like the idea much. The lounger in him did not enjoy the thought of London. Gradually his mind wandered away into scheming—infinite scheming—what would he do if he went, what would he do if he did not go?

A beetle, attracted by the faint sunlight, had crawled out of its hole. It saw the paper and crept on to it, the better to catch the sunlight. Sherman saw the beetle but his mind was not occupied with it. 'Shall I tell Mary Carton?' he was thinking. Mary had long been his adviser and friend. She was, indeed, everybody's adviser. Yes, he would ask her what to do. Then again he thought—no, he would decide for himself. The beetle began to move. 'If it goes off the paper by the top I will ask her—if by the bottom I will not.'

The beetle went off by the top. He got up with an air of decision and went into the tool-house and began sorting seeds and picking out the light ones, sometimes stopping to watch a spider; for he knew he must wait till the afternoon to see Mary Carton. The tool-house was a favourite place with him. He often read there and watched the spiders in the corners.

At dinner he was preoccupied.

'Mother,' he said, 'would you mind much if we went away from this?'

4. NY: . . . revery, . . . .      if he did not go.
11. NY: . . . go? Would he . . . .     17. L, NY: . . . of his hole.
14. L, NY: . . . what he would do     18. NY: . . . bettle, but . . . .
    if he went, what he would do

'I have often told you,' she answered, 'I do not like one place better than another. I like them all equally little.'

After dinner he went again into the tool-house. This time he did not sort seeds—only watched the spiders.

## III

Towards evening he went out. The pale sunshine of winter flickered on his path. The wind blew the straws about. He grew more and more melancholy. A dog of his acquaintance was chasing rabbits in a field. He had never been known to catch one, and since his youth had never seen one, for he was almost wholly blind. They were his form of the eternal chimera. The dog left the field and followed with a friendly sniff.

They came together to the rectory. Mary Carton was not in. There was a children's practice in the school-house. They went thither.

A child of four or five with a swelling on its face was sitting under a wall opposite the school door, waiting to make faces at the Protestant children as they came out. Catching sight of the dog she seemed to debate in her mind whether to throw a stone at it or call it to her. She threw the stone and made it run. In after times he remembered all these things as though they were of importance.

He opened the latched green door and went in. About twenty children were singing in shrill voices, standing in a row at the further end. At the harmonium he recognised Mary Carton, who nodded to him and went on with her playing. The whitewashed walls were covered with glazed prints of animals; at the further end was a large map of Europe; by a fire at the near end was a table with the remains of tea. This tea was an idea of Mary's. They had

5. NY: Toward evening . . . .
10. L, NY: . . . one for . . . .
14. NY: . . . schoolhouse.
24. L, NY: . . . voices standing . . . .
25. L, NY: . . . recognized . . . .
27. L: . . . white-washed . . . .

tea and cake first, afterwards the singing. The floor was covered with crumbs. The fire was burning brightly. Sherman sat down beside it. A child with a great deal of oil in her hair was sitting on the end of a form at the other side.

'Look,' she whispered, 'I have been sent away. At any rate they are further from the fire. They have to be near the harmonium. I would not sing. Do you like hymns? I don't. Will you have a cup of tea? I can make it quite well. See, I did not spill a drop. Have you enough milk?' It was a cup full of milk—children's tea. 'Look, there is a mouse carrying away a crumb. Hush!'

They sat there, the child watching the mouse, Sherman pondering on his letter, until the music ceased and the children came tramping down the room. The mouse having fled, Sherman's self-appointed hostess got up with a sigh and went out with the others.

Mary Carton closed the harmonium and came towards Sherman. Her face and all her movements showed a gentle decision of character. Her glance was serene, her features regular, her figure at the same time ample and beautifully moulded; her dress plain yet not without a certain air of distinction. In a different society she would have had many suitors. But she was of a type that in country towns does not get married at all. Its beauty is too lacking in pink and white, its nature in that small assertiveness admired for character by the uninstructed. Elsewhere she would have known her own beauty—as it is right that all the beautiful should—and have learnt how to display it, to add gesture to her calm and more of mirth and smiles to her grave cheerfulness. As it was, her manner was much older than herself.

She sat down by Sherman with the air of an old friend. They had long been accustomed to consult together on every matter. They were such good friends they had never fallen in love with each other. Perfect love and perfect friendship are indeed incompatible; for the one is a battle-

1. NY: . . . afterward . . . .     21. NY: . . . molded; . . . .
17. NY: . . . toward . . . .

field where shadows war beside the combatants, and the other a placid country where Consultation has her dwelling.

These two were such good friends that the most gossiping townspeople had given them up with a sigh. The doctor's wife, a faded beauty and devoted romance reader, said one day, as they passed, 'They are such cold creatures'; the old maid who kept the Berlin-wool shop remarked, 'They are not of the marrying sort'; and now their comings and goings were no longer noticed. Nothing had ever come to break in on their quiet companionship and give obscurity as a dwelling-place for the needed illusions. Had one been weak and the other strong, one plain and the other handsome, one guide and the other guided, one wise and the other foolish, love might have found them out in a moment, for love is based on inequality as friendship is on equality.

'John,' said Mary Carton, warming her hands at the fire, 'I have had a troublesome day. Did you come to help me teach the children to sing? It was good of you: you were just too late.'

'No,' he answered, 'I have come to be your pupil. I am always your pupil.'

'Yes, and a most disobedient one.'

'Well, advise me this time at any rate. My uncle has written, offering me a hundred pounds a year to begin with in his London office. Am I to go?'

'You know quite well my answer,' she said.

'Indeed I do not. Why should I go? I am contented here. I am now making my garden ready for spring. Later on there will be trout fishing and saunters by the edge of the river in the evening when the bats are flickering about. In July there will be races. I enjoy the bustle. I enjoy life here. When anything annoys me I keep away from it, that is all. You know I am always busy. I have occupation and

7. *L*, *NY*: . . . creatures.'  26. *L*, *NY*: . . . me £100 a
    The . . .      year . . . .
9. *L*, *NY*: . . . sort,' and . . . .  31. *NY*: . . . trout-fishing . . . .
20. *NY*: . . . you; you . . . .

friends and am quite contented.'

'It is a great loss to many of us, but you must go, John,' she said. 'For you know you will be old some day, and perhaps when the vitality of youth is gone you will feel that your life is empty and find that you are too old to change it; and you will give up, perhaps, trying to be happy and likeable and become as the rest are. I think I can see you,' she said, with a laugh, 'a hypochondriac, like Gorman, the retired excise officer, or with a red nose like Dr. Stephens, or growing like Peters, the elderly cattle merchant, who starves his horse.'

'They were bad material to begin with,' he answered, 'and, besides, I cannot take my mother away with me at her age, and I cannot leave her alone.'

'What annoyance it may be,' she answered, 'will soon be forgotten. You will be able to give her many more comforts. We women—we all like to be dressed well and have pleasant rooms to sit in, and a young man at your age should not be idle. You must go away from this little backward place. We shall miss you, but you are clever and must go and work with other men and have your talents admitted.'

'How emulous you would have me! Perhaps I shall be well-to-do some day; meanwhile I only wish to stay here with my friends.'

She went over to the window and looked out with her face turned from him. The evening light cast a long shadow behind her on the floor. After some moments, she said, 'I see people ploughing on the slope of the hill. There are people working on a house to the right. Everywhere there are people busy,' and with a slight tremble in her voice she added, 'and, John, nowhere are there any doing what they wish. One has to think of so many things—of duty and God.'

'Mary, I didn't know you were so religious.'

8. NY: . . . hypochondriac like . . . .
13. L, NY: . . . 'and besides, . . . .
23. L, NY: . . . have me.

29. NY: . . . plowing . . . .
31. L, NY: . . . and, with a slight tremble in her voice, she . . . .

Coming towards him with a smile, she said, 'No more did I, perhaps. But sometimes the self in one is very strong. One has to think a great deal and reason with it. Yet I try hard to lose myself in things about me. These children now —I often lie awake thinking about them. That child who was talking to you is often on my mind. I do not know what will happen to her. She makes me unhappy. I am afraid she is not a good child at all. I am afraid she is not taught well at home. I try hard to be gentle and patient with her. I am a little displeased with myself to-day, so I have lectured you. There! I have made my confession. But,' she added, taking one of his hands in both hers and reddening, 'you must go away. You must not be idle. You will gain everything.'

As she stood there with bright eyes, the light of evening about her, Sherman for perhaps the first time saw how beautiful she was, and was flattered by her interest. For the first time also her presence did not make him at peace with the world.

'Will you be an obedient pupil?'

'You know so much more than I do,' he answered, 'and are so much wiser. I will write to my uncle and agree to his offer.'

'Now you must go home,' she said. 'You must not keep your mother waiting for her tea. There! I have raked the fire out. We must not forget to lock the door behind us.'

As they stood on the doorstep the wind blew a whirl of dead leaves about them.

'They are my old thoughts,' he said; 'see, they are all withered.'

They walked together silently. At the vicarage he left her and went homeward.

The deserted flour-store at the corner of two roads, the house that had been burnt hollow ten years before and still lifted its blackened beams, the straggling and leafless fruit-trees rising above garden walls, the church where he was

---

1. NY: . . . toward . . . .      33. L, NY: . . . flour store . . .
10. L, NY: . . . to-day; so . . . .   35. NY; . . . fruit trees . . . .

christened—these foster-mothers of his infancy seemed to nod and shake their heads over him.

'Mother,' he said, hurriedly entering the room, 'we are going to London.'

'As you wish. I always knew you would be a rolling stone,' she answered, and went out to tell the servant that as soon as she had finished the week's washing they must pack up everything, for they were going to London.

'Yes, we must pack up,' said the old peasant; she did not stop peeling the onion in her hand—she had not comprehended. In the middle of the night she suddenly started up in bed with a pale face and a prayer to the Virgin whose image hung over her head—she had now comprehended.


## IV


On January the 5th, about two in the afternoon, Sherman sat on the deck of the steamer *Lavinia* enjoying a period of sunshine between two showers. The steamer *Lavinia* was a cattle-boat. It had been his wish to travel by some more expensive route, but his mother, with her old-fashioned ideas of duty, would not hear of it, and now, as he foresaw, was extremely uncomfortable below, while he, who was a good sailor, was pretty happy on deck, and would have been quite so if the pigs would only tire of their continual squealing. With the exception of a very dirty old woman sitting by a crate of geese, all the passengers but himself were below. This old woman made the journey monthly with geese for the Liverpool market.

Sherman was dreaming. He began to feel very desolate, and commenced a letter to Mary Carton in his notebook to state this fact. He was a laborious and unpractised writer, and found it helped him to make a pencil copy. Sometimes he stopped and watched the puffin sleeping on the waves.

14. L, NY: . . . 5th about . . . .    28. NY: . . . notebook, to . . . .
17. L: . . . cattle boat.              29. NY: . . . unpracticed . . . .

Each one of them had its head tucked in in a somewhat different way. 'That is because their characters are different,' he thought.

Gradually he began to notice a great many corks floating by, one after the other. The old woman saw them too, and said, waking out of a half sleep: 'Misther John Sherman, we will be in the Mersey before evening. Why are ye goin' among them savages in London, Misther John? Why don't ye stay among your own people—for what have we in this life but a mouthful of air?'

2. *L:* . . . way. That . . . .
*NY:* [New paragraph begins here.]

6. *L:* . . . sleep— . . .
6. *L, NY:* [New paragraph begins here.]

# MARGARET LELAND

## I

Sherman and his mother rented a small house on the north side of St. Peter's Square, Hammersmith. The front windows looked out on to the old rank and green square, the windows behind on to a little patch of garden round which the houses gathered and pressed as though they already longed to trample it out. In this garden was a single tall pear tree that never bore fruit.

Three years passed by without any notable event. Sherman went every day to his office in Tower Hill Street, abused his work a great deal, and was not unhappy perhaps. He was probably a bad clerk, but then nobody was very exacting with the nephew of the head of the firm.

The firm of Sherman and Saunders, ship-brokers, was a long-established, old-fashioned house. Saunders had been dead some years and old Michael Sherman ruled alone —an old bachelor full of family pride and pride in his wealth. He lived, for all that, in a very simple fashion. His mahogany furniture was a little solider than other people's perhaps. He did not understand display. Display finds its

1. NY: On the north side of St. Peter's Square, Hammersmith, Sherman and his mother rented a small house.
7. L: . . . pear-tree . . . .       13. L, NY: . . . ship brokers,
. . . .

excuse in some taste good or bad, and in a long industrious life Michael Sherman had never found leisure to form one. He seemed to live only from habit. Year by year he grew more silent, gradually ceasing to regard anything but his family and his ships. His family were represented by his nephew and his nephew's mother. He did not feel much affection for them. He believed in his family—that was all. To remind him of the other goal of his thoughts hung round his private office pictures with such inscriptions as 'S.S. *Indus* at the Cape of Good Hope,' 'The barque *Mary* in the Mozambique Channel,' 'The barque *Livingstone* at Port Said,' and many more. Every rope was drawn accurately with a ruler, and here and there were added distant vessels sailing proudly by with all that indifference to perspective peculiar to the drawings of sailors. On every ship was the flag of the firm spread out to show the letters.

No man cared for old Michael Sherman. Every one liked John. Both were silent, but the young man had sometimes a talkative fit. The old man lived for his ledger, the young man for his dreams.

In spite of all these differences, the uncle was on the whole pleased with the nephew. He noticed a certain stolidity that was of the family. It sometimes irritated others. It pleased him. He saw a hundred indications besides that made him say, 'He is a true Sherman. We Shermans begin that way and give up frivolity as we grow old. We are all the same in the end.'


Mrs. Sherman and her son had but a small round of acquaintances—a few rich people, clients of the house of Sherman and Saunders for the most part. Among these was a Miss Margaret Leland who lived with her mother, the widow of the late Henry Leland, ship-broker, on the eastern side of St. Peter's Square. Their house was larger than the Shermans', and noticeable among its fellows by the newly-

1. NY: . . . taste, good . . . .     34. L: . . . Shermans, . . .
32. NY: . . . ship broker, . . . .

*61*

painted hall-door. Within on every side were bronzes and china vases and heavy curtains. In all were displayed the curious and vagrant taste of Margaret Leland: the rich Italian and mediaeval draperies of pre-Raphaelite taste jostling the brightest and vulgarest products of more native and Saxon schools; vases of the most artistic shape and colour side by side with artificial flowers and stuffed birds. This house belonged to the Lelands. They had bought it in less prosperous days, and having altered it according to their taste and the need of their growing welfare could not decide to leave it.

Sherman was an occasional caller at the Lelands, and had certainly a liking, though not a very deep one, for Margaret. As yet he knew little more about her than that she wore the most fascinating hats, that the late Lord Lytton was her favourite author, and that she hated frogs. It is clear that she did not know that a French writer on magic says the luxurious and extravagant hate frogs because they are cold, solitary, and dreary.[5] Had she done so, she would have been more cautious about revealing her tastes.

For the rest, John Sherman was forgetting the town of Ballah. He corresponded indeed with Mary Carton, but his laborious letter-writing made his letters fewer and fewer. Sometimes, too, he heard from Howard, who had a curacy at Glasgow and was on indifferent terms with his parishioners. They objected to his way of conducting the services. His letters were full of it. He would not give in, he said, whatever happened. His conscience was involved.

## II

One afternoon Mrs. Leland called on Mrs. Sherman. She very often called—this fat, sentimental woman, moving in the midst of a cloud of scent. The day was warm, and

1. L: . . . hall door.
   NY: . . . newly painted hall door.
3. L, NY: . . . Leland. The . . .
4. L, NY: . . . of the pre-Raphaelites jostling . . .
6. L, NY: . . . schools. Vases . . .
7. NY: . . . color . . . .
20. L, NY: . . . more circumspect about . . . .
21. L, NY: . . . rest John . . . .
23. L, NY: . . . letter writing . . . .

she carried her too elaborate and heavy dress as a large caddis-fly drags its case with much labour and patience. She sat down on the sofa with obvious relief, leaning so heavily among the cushions that a clothes-moth fluttered out of an antimacassar, to be knocked down and crushed by Mrs. Sherman, who was very quick in her movements.

As soon as she found her breath, Mrs. Leland began a long history of her sorrows. Her daughter Margaret had been jilted and was in despair, had taken to her bed with every resolution to die, and was growing paler and paler. The hard-hearted man, though she knew he had heard, did not relent. She knew he had heard because her daughter had told his sister all about it, and his sister had no heart, because she said it was temper that ailed Margaret, and she was a little vixen, and that if she had not flirted with everybody the engagement would never have been broken off. But Mr. Sims had no heart clearly, as Miss Marriot and Mrs. Eliza Taylor, her daughter's friends, said, when they heard, and Lock, the butler, said the same too, and Mary Young, the house-maid, said so too—and she knew all about it, for Margaret used to read his letters to her often when having her hair brushed.

'She must have been very fond of him,' said Mrs. Sherman.

'She is so romantic, my dear,' answered Mrs. Leland, with a sigh. 'I am afraid she takes after an uncle on her father's side, who wrote poetry and wore a velvet jacket and ran away with an Italian countess who used to get drunk. When I married Mr. Leland people said he was not worthy of me, and that I was throwing myself away—and he in business, too! But Margaret is so romantic. There was Mr. Walters, a gentleman-farmer, and Simpson who had a jeweller's shop—I never approved of him!—and Mr. Samuelson, and the Hon. William Scott. She tired of them all

2. NY: . . . case, with . . .
2. NY: . . . labor . . . .
4. L, NY: . . . clothes-moth in an antimacassar thought the end of the world had come and fluttered out only to . . . .

8. L: . . . Margaret, had . . . .
32. L, NY: . . . Walters, the gentleman farmer, . . .
32. NY: . . . Simpson, who . . . .

except the Hon. William Scott, who tired of her because someone told him she put belladonna in her eyes—and it is not true; and now there is Mr. Sims!' She then cried a little, and allowed herself to be consoled by Mrs. Sherman.

'You talk so intelligently and are so well informed,' she said at parting. 'I have made a very pleasant call,' and the caddis-worm toiled upon its way, arriving in time at other cups of tea.

## III

The day after Mrs. Leland's call upon his mother, John Sherman, returning home after his not very lengthy day in the office, saw Margaret coming towards him. She had a lawn-tennis racket under her arm, and was walking slowly on the shady side of the road. She was a pretty girl with quite irregular features, who though not really more than pretty, had so much manner, so much of an air, that every one called her a beauty: a trefoil with the fragance of a rose.

'Mr. Sherman,' she cried, coming smiling to meet him, 'I have been ill, but could not stand the house any longer. I am going to the Square to play tennis. Will you come with me?'

'I am a bad player,' he said.

'Of course you are,' she answered; 'but you are the only person under a hundred to be found this afternoon. How dull life is!' she continued, with a sigh. 'You heard how ill I have been? What do you do all day?'

'I sit at a desk, sometimes writing, and sometimes, when I get lazy, looking up at the flies. There are fourteen on the plaster of the ceiling over my head. They died two winters ago. I sometimes think to have them brushed off, but they have been there so long now I hardly like to.'

'Ah! you like them,' she said, 'because you are accustomed to them. In most cases there is not much more to be

2. L, NY: . . . some one . . . .
7. L, NY: . . . arriving in due course at . . . .
11. NY: . . . toward . . . .
12. L: . . . lawn tennis . . . .
14. L, NY: . . . though really not more . . . .

said for our family affections, I think.'

'In a room close at hand,' he went on, 'there is, you know, Uncle Michael, who never speaks.'

'Precisely. You have an uncle who never speaks; I have a mother who never is silent. She went to see Mrs. Sherman the other day. What did she say to her?'

'Nothing.'

'Really! What a dull thing existence is!'—this with a great sigh. 'When the Fates are weaving our web of life some mischievous goblin always runs off with the dye-pot. Everything is dull and grey. Am I looking a little pale? I have been so very ill.'

'A little bit pale, perhaps,' he said, doubtfully.

The Square gate brought them to a stop. It was locked, but she had the key. The lock was stiff, but turned easily for John Sherman.

'How strong you are,' she said.

It was an iridescent evening of spring. The leaves of the bushes had still their faint green. As Margaret darted about at the tennis, a red feather in her cap seemed to rejoice with its wearer. Everything was at once gay and tranquil. The whole world had that unreal air it assumes at beautiful moments, as though it might vanish at a touch like an iridescent soap-bubble.

After a little Margaret said she was tired, and, sitting on a garden-seat among the bushes, began telling him the plots of novels lately read by her. Suddenly she cried: 'The novel-writers were all serious people like you. They are so hard on people like me. They always make us come to a bad end. They *say* we are always acting, acting, acting; and what else do you serious people do? You act before the world. I think, do you know, *we* act before ourselves. All the old foolish kings and queens in history were like us. They laughed and beckoned and went to the block for no

8. *L, NY:* 'Really. What . . . .    27. *L:* . . . cried—. . .
11. *NY:* . . . gray.                *L, NY:* [New paragraph be-
13. *NY:* . . . said doubtfully.     gins here.]
26. *L, NY:* . . . garden seat . . . .    28. *NY:* . . . novel writers . . . .

**65**

very good purpose. I daresay the headsmen were like you.'

'We would never cut off so pretty a head.'

'Oh, yes, you would—you would cut off mine to-morrow.' All this she said vehemently, piercing him with her bright eyes. 'You would cut off my head to-morrow,' she repeated, almost fiercely; 'I tell you you would.'

Her departure was always unexpected, her moods changed with so much rapidity. 'Look!' she said, pointing where the clock on St. Peter's church showed above the bushes. 'Five minutes to five. In five minutes my mother's tea-hour. It is like growing old. I go to gossip. Good-bye.'

The red feather shone for a moment among the bushes and was gone.

## IV

The next day and the day after, Sherman was followed by those bright eyes. When he opened a letter at his desk they seemed to gaze at him from the open paper, and to watch him from the flies upon the ceiling. He was even a worse clerk than usual.

One evening he said to his mother, 'Miss Leland has beautiful eyes.'

'My dear, she puts belladonna in them.'

'What a thing to say!'

'I know she does, though her mother denies it.'

'Well, she is certainly beautiful,' he answered.

'My dear, if she has an attraction for you, I don't want to discourage it. She is rich as girls go nowadays; and one woman has one fault, another another: one's untidy, one fights with her servants, one fights with her friends, another has a crabbed tongue when she talks of them.'

Sherman became again silent, finding no fragment of romance in such a discourse.

12. NY: Good-by.'          32. *L*, **NY**: . . . such discourse.

In the next week or two he saw much of Miss Leland. He met her almost every evening on his return from the office, walking slowly, her racket under her arm. They played tennis much and talked more. Sherman began to play tennis in his dreams. Miss Leland told him all about herself, her friends, her inmost feelings; and yet every day he knew less about her. It was not merely that saying everything she said nothing, but that continually there came through her wild words the sound of the mysterious flutes and viols of that unconscious nature which dwells so much nearer to woman than to man. How often do we not endow the beautiful and candid with depth and mystery not their own? We do not know that we but hear in their voices those flutes and viols playing to us of the alluring secret of the world.

Sherman had never known in early life what is called first love, and now, when he had passed thirty, it came to him—that love more of the imagination than of either the senses or affections: it was mainly the eyes that followed him.

It is not to be denied that as this love grew serious it grew mercenary. Now active, now latent, the notion had long been in Sherman's mind, as we know, that he should marry money. A born lounger, riches tempted him greatly. When those eyes haunted him from the fourteen flies on the ceiling, he would say, 'I should be rich; I should have a house in the country; I should hunt and shoot, and have a garden and three gardeners; I should leave this abominable office.' Then the eyes became even more beautiful. It was a new kind of belladonna.

He shrank a little, however, from choosing even this pleasant pathway. He had planned many futures for himself and learnt to love them all. It was this that had made him linger on at Ballah for so long, and it was this that now kept him undecided. He would have to give up the universe for a garden and three gardeners. How sad it was to make

6. NY: . . . herself; her . . . .    18. L: . . . him that . . . .
                                         NY: . . . him, that . . . .

substantial even the best of dreams. How hard it was to submit to that decree which compels every step we take in life to be a death in the imagination. How difficult it was to be so enwrapped in this one new hope as not to hear the lamentations that were going on in dim corners of his mind.

One day he resolved to propose. He examined himself in the glass in the morning; and for the first time in his life smiled to see how good-looking he was. In the evening before leaving the office he peered at himself in the mirror over the mantlepiece in the room where customers were received. The sun was blazing through the window full on his face. He did not look so well. Immediately all courage left him.

That evening he went out after his mother had gone to bed and walked far along the towing-path of the Thames. A faint mist half covered away the houses and factory chimneys on the further side; beside him a band of osiers swayed softly, the deserted and full river lapping their stems. He looked on all these things with foreign eyes. He had no sense of possession. Indeed it seemed to him that everything in London was owned by too many to be owned by anyone. Another river that he did seem to possess flowed through his memory with all its familiar sights—boys riding in the stream to the saddle-girths, fish leaping, water-flies raising their small ripples, a swan asleep, the wallflowers growing on the red brick of the margin. He grew very sad. Suddenly a shooting star, fiery and vagabond, leaped from the darkness. It brought his mind again in a moment to Margaret Leland. To marry her, he thought, was to separate himself from the old life he loved so well.

Crossing the river at Putney, he hurried homewards among the market-gardens. Nearing home, the streets were deserted, the shops closed. Where King Street joins the Broadway, entirely alone with itself, in the very centre of

11. NY: . . . mantelpiece . . . .      33. L, NY: . . . market gardens.
23. L: . . . any one.                         35. NY: . . . center . . . .
32. NY: . . . homeward . . .

68

the road a little black cat was leaping after its shadow.

'Ah!' he thought, 'it would be a good thing to be a little black cat. To leap about in the moonlight and sleep in the sunlight, and catch flies, to have no hard tasks to do or hard decisions to come to, to be simple and full of animal spirits.'[8]

At the corner of Bridge Road was a coffee-stall, the only sign of human life. He bought some cold meat and flung it to the little black cat.

# V

Some more days went by. At last, one day, arriving at the Square somewhat earlier than usual, and sitting down to wait for Margaret on the seat among the bushes, he noticed the pieces of a torn-up letter lying about. Beside him on the seat was a pencil, as though someone had been writing there and left it behind them. The pencil-lead was worn very short. The letter had been torn up, perhaps in a fit of impatience.

In a half-mechanical way he glanced over the scraps. On one of them he read: 'MY DEAR ELIZA,— What an incurable gossip my mother is. You heard of my misfortune. I nearly died——' Here he had to search among the scraps; at last he found one that seemed to follow. 'Perhaps you will hear news from me soon. There is a handsome young man who pays me attention, and——' Here another piece had to be found. 'I would take him though he had a face like the man in the moon, and limped like the devil at the theatre. Perhaps I am a little in love. Oh! friend of my heart—' Here it broke off again. He was interested, and searched the grass and the bushes for fragments. Some had been blown to quite a distance. He got together several sentences now. 'I will not spend another winter with my

10. NY: A few more . . . .    19. NY: . . . ELIZA: What . . . .
16. L, NY: . . . up, perhaps,    27. NY: . . . theater.
   in . . . .

mother for anything. All this is, of course, a secret. I had to tell somebody; secrets are bad for my health. Perhaps it will all come to nothing.' Then the letter went off into dress, the last novel the writer had read, and so forth. A Miss Sims, too, was mentioned, who had said some unkind thing of the writer.

Sherman was greatly amused. It did not seem to him wrong to read—we do not mind spying on one of the crowd, any more than on the personages of literature. It never occurred to him that he, or any friend of his, was concerned in these pencil scribblings.

Suddenly he saw this sentence: 'Heigho! your poor Margaret is falling in love again; condole with her, my dear.'

He started. The name 'Margaret,' the mention of Miss Sims, the style of the whole letter, all made plain the authorship. Very desperately ashamed of himself, he got up and tore each scrap of paper into still smaller fragments and scattered them far apart.

That evening he proposed and was accepted.

## VI

For several days there was a new heaven and a new earth. Miss Leland seemed suddenly impressed with the seriousness of life. She was gentleness itself; and as Sherman sat on Sunday mornings in his pocket-handkerchief of a garden under the one tree, with its smoky stem, watching the little circles of sunlight falling from the leaves like a shower of new sovereigns, he gazed at them with a longer and keener joy than heretofore—a new heaven and a new earth, surely!

Sherman planted and dug and raked this pocket-handkerchief of a garden most diligently, rooting out the docks and dandelions and mouse-ear and the patches of untimely

20. L, NY: . . . proposed, and . . . .

70

grass. It was the point of contact between his new life and the old. It was far too small and unfertile and shaded-in to satisfy his love of gardener's experiments and early vegetables. Perforce this husbandry was too little complex for his affections to gather much round plant and bed. His garden in Ballah used to touch him like the growth of a young family. Now he was content to satisfy his barbaric sense of colour; right round were planted alternate hollyhock and sunflower, and behind them scarlet-runners showed their inch-high cloven shoots.

One Sunday it occurred to him to write to his friends on the matter of his engagement. He numbered them over. Howard, one or two less intimate, and Mary Carton. At that name he paused; he would not write just yet.

## VII

One Saturday there was a tennis party. Miss Leland devoted herself all day to a young Foreign Office clerk. She played tennis with him, talked with him, drank lemonade with him, had neither thoughts nor words for anyone else. John Sherman was quite happy. Tennis was always a bore, and now he was not called upon to play. It had not struck him there was occasion for jealousy.

As the guests were dispersing, his betrothed came to him. Her manner seemed strange.

'Does anything ail you, Margaret?' he asked, as they left the Square.

'Everything,' she answered, looking about her with ostentatious secrecy. 'You are a most annoying person. You have no feeling; you have no temperament; you are quite the most stupid creature I was ever engaged to.'

'What is wrong with you?' he asked, in bewilderment.

2. L, NY: . . . shaded in . . . .
4. L, NY: [New paragraph begins here.]
7. L, NY: [New paragraph begins here.]

8. NY: . . . color . . . .
8. L: . . . holyhock . . . .
18. L: . . . any one . . . .

'Don't you see,' she replied, with a broken voice, 'I flirted all day with that young clerk? You should have nearly killed me with jealousy. You do not love me a bit! There is no knowing what I might do!'

'Well, you know,' he said, 'It was not right of you. People might say, "Look at John Sherman; how furious he must be!" To be sure, I wouldn't be furious a bit; but then they'd go about saying I was. It would not matter, of course; but you know it is not right of you.'

'It is no use pretending you have feeling. It is all that miserable little town you come from, with its sleepy old shops and its sleepy old society. I would give up loving you this minute,' she added, with a caressing look, 'if you had not that beautiful bronzed face. I will improve you. To-morrow evening you must come to the opera.' Suddenly she changed the subject. 'Do you see that little fat man coming out of the Square and staring at me? I was engaged to him once. Look at the four old ladies behind him, shaking their bonnets at me. Each has some story about me, and it will all be the same in a hundred years.'

After this he had hardly a moment's peace. She kept him continually going to theatres, operas, parties. These last were an especial trouble; for it was her wont to gather about her an admiring circle to listen to her extravagancies, and he was no longer at the age when we enjoy audacity for its own sake.

## VIII

Gradually those bright eyes of his imagination, watching him from letters and from among the fourteen flies on the ceiling, had ceased to be centres of peace. They seemed like two whirlpools, wherein the order and quiet of his life were absorbed hourly and daily.

He still thought sometimes of the country house of his

7. L, NY: . . . sure I . . . .        29. NY: . . . centers . . . .
22. NY: . . . theaters, . . . .

dreams and of the garden and the three gardeners, but somehow they had lost half their charm.

He had written to Howard and some others, and commenced, at last, a letter to Mary Carton. It lay unfinished on his desk; a thin coating of dust was gathering upon it.

Mrs. Leland called continually on Mrs. Sherman. She sentimentalized over the lovers, and even wept over them; each visit supplied the household with conversation for a week.

Every Sunday morning—his letter-writing time—Sherman looked at his uncompleted letter. Gradually it became plain to him he could not finish it. It had never seemed to him he had more than friendship for Mary Carton, yet somehow it was not possible to tell her of this love-affair.

The more his betrothed troubled him the more he thought about the unfinished letter. He was a man standing at the cross roads.

Whenever the wind blew from the south he remembered his friend, for that is the wind that fills the heart with memory.

One Sunday he removed the dust from the face of the letter almost reverently, as though it were the dust from the wheels of destiny. But the letter remained unfinished.

## IX

One Wednesday in June Sherman arrived home an hour earlier than usual from his office, as his wont was the first Wednesday in every month, on which day his mother was at home to her friends. They had not many callers. To-day there was no one as yet but a badly-dressed old lady his mother had picked up he knew not where. She had been looking at his photograph album, and recalling names and dates from her own prosperous times. As she went out Miss Leland came in. She gave the old lady in passing a critical

17. *L*, NY: . . . cross-roads.      28. NY: . . . badly dressed . . . .

look that made the poor creature very conscious of a threadbare mantle, and went over to Mrs. Sherman, holding out both hands. Sherman, who knew all his mother's peculiarities, noticed on her side a slight coldness; perhaps she did not altogether like this beautiful dragon-fly.

'I have come,' said Miss Leland, 'to tell John that he must learn to paint. Music and society are not enough. There is nothing like art to give refinement.' Then turning to John Sherman—'My dear, I will make you quite different. You are a dreadful barbarian, you know.'

'What ails me, Margaret?'

'Just look at that necktie! Nothing shows a man's cultivation like his necktie! Then your reading! You never read anything but old books nobody wants to talk about. I will lend you three everyone has read this month. You really must acquire small talk and change your necktie.'

Presently she noticed the photograph-book lying open on a chair.

'Oh!' she cried, 'I must have another look at John's beauties.'

It was a habit of his to gather all manner of pretty faces. It came from incipient old bachelorhood, perhaps.

Margaret criticised each photograph in turn with, 'Ah! she looks as if she had some life in her!' or 'I do not like your sleepy eyelids,' or some such phrase. The mere relations were passed by without a word. One face occurred several times—a quiet face. As Margaret came on this one for the third time, Mrs. Sherman, who seemed a little resentful about something, said: 'That is his friend, Mary Carton.'

'He told me about her. He has a book she gave him. So that is she? How interesting! I pity these poor country people. It must be hard to keep from getting stupid.'

'My friend is not at all stupid,' said Sherman.

'Does she speak with a brogue? I remember you told me

9. NY: . . . Sherman: 'My . . . .
15. L: . . . every one . . . .
16. NY: . . . small-talk . . . .
23. L: . . . criticized . . .
23. L, NY: . . . each photo in . . .
24. L, NY: . . . or, 'I . . . .
29. L: . . . said—. . .
L, NY: [New paragraph begins here.]
31. NY: . . . country-people.

she was very good. It must be difficult to keep from talking platitudes when one is very good.'

'You are quite wrong about her. You would like her very much,' he replied.

'She is one of those people, I suppose, who can only talk about their relatives, or their families, or about their friends' children: how this one has got the whooping-cough, and this one is getting well of the measles!' She kept swaying one of the leaves between her finger and thumb impatiently. 'What a strange way she does her hair; and what an ugly dress!'

'You must not talk that way about her—she is my great friend.'

'Friend! friend!' she burst out. 'He thinks I will believe in friendship between a man and a woman!'

She got up, and said, turning round with an air of changing the subject, 'Have you written to your friends about our engagement? You had not done so when I asked you lately.'

'I have.'

'All?'

'Well, not all.'

'Your great friend, Miss——what do you call her?'

'Miss Carton. I have not written to her.'

She tapped impatiently with her foot.

'They were really old companions—that is all,' said Mrs. Sherman, wishing to mend matters. 'They were both readers; that brought them together. I never much fancied her. Yet she was well enough as a friend, and helped, maybe, with reading, and the gardening, and his good bringing-up, to keep him from the idle young men of the neighbourhood.'

'You must make him write and tell her at once—you must, you must!' almost sobbed out Miss Leland.

'I promise,' he answered.

Immediately returning to herself, she cried, 'If I were in

7. L: . . . hooping-cough, . . . .   16. NY: . . . up and . . . .
15. L, NY: . . . a woman.'   32. NY: . . . neighborhood.

75

her place I know what I would like to do when I got the
letter. I know who I would like to kill!'—this with a laugh
as she went over and looked at herself in the mirror on the
mantlepiece.

3. L: . . . over, and . . .          the . . .
3. L, NY: . . . mirror over       4. NY: . . . mantelpiece.

# JOHN SHERMAN REVISITS BALLAH

## I

The others had gone, and Sherman was alone in the drawing-room by himself, looking through the window. Never had London seemed to him so like a reef whereon he was cast away. In the Square the bushes were covered with dust; some sparrows were ruffling their feathers on the side-walk; people passed, continually disturbing them. The sky was full of smoke. A terrible feeling of solitude in the midst of a multitude oppressed him. A portion of his life was ending. He thought that soon he would be no longer a young man, and now, at the period when the desire of novelty grows less, was coming the great change of his life. He felt he was of those whose granaries are in the past. And now this past would never renew itself. He was going out into the distance as though with strange sailors in a strange ship.

He longed to see again the town where he had spent his childhood: to see the narrow roads and mean little shops. And perhaps it would be easier to tell her who had been the friend of so many years of this engagement in his own

6. NY: . . . sidewalk; . . . .     17. NY: . . . road . . . .

person than by letter. He wondered why it was so hard to write so simple a thing.

It was his custom to act suddenly on his decisions. He had not made many in his life. The next day he announced at the office that he would be absent for three or four days. He told his mother he had business in the country.

His betrothed met him on the way to the terminus, as he was walking, bag in hand, and asked where he was going. 'I am going on business to the country,' he said, and blushed. He was creeping away like a thief.

## II

He arrived in the town of Ballah by rail, for he had avoided the slow cattle-steamer and gone by Dublin.

It was the forenoon, and he made for the Imperial Hotel to wait till four in the evening, when he would find Mary Carton in the schoolhouse, for he had timed his journey so as to arrive on Thursday, the day of the children's practice.

As he went through the streets his heart went out to every familiar place and sight: the rows of tumble-down thatched cottages; the slated roofs of the shops; the women selling gooseberries; the river bridge; the high walls of the garden where it was said the gardener used to see the ghost of a former owner in the shape of a rabbit; the street corner no child would pass at nightfall for fear of the headless soldier; the deserted flour-store; the wharves covered with grass. All these he watched with Celtic devotion, that devotion carried to the ends of the world by the Celtic exiles, and since old time surrounding their journeyings with rumour of plaintive songs.

He sat in the window of the Imperial Hotel, now full of guests. He did not notice any of them. He sat there meditating, meditating. Grey clouds covering the town

8. NY: . . . walking bag . . . .
9. NY: . . . said and . . . .
11. NY: The town of Ballah he reached by rail, . . .
12. L, NY: . . . cattle steamer . . . .
24. L, NY: . . . flour store; . . . .
27. NY: . . . rumor . . . .
31. NY: Gray . . . .

with flying shadows rushed by like the old and dishevelled eagles that Maeldune saw hurrying towards the waters of life.[7] Below in the street passed by country people, townspeople, travellers, women with baskets, boys driving donkeys, old men with sticks; sometimes he recognized a face or was recognized himself, and welcomed by some familiar voice.

'You have come home a handsomer gentleman than your father, Misther John, and he was a neat figure of a man, God bless him!' said the waiter, bringing him his lunch; and in truth Sherman had grown handsomer for these years away. His face and gesture had more of dignity, for on the centre of his nature life had dropped a pinch of experience.

At four he left the hotel and waited near the schoolhouse till the children came running out. One or two of the elder ones he recognized but turned away.

## III

Mary Carton was locking the harmonium as he went in. She came to meet him with a surprised and joyful air.

'How often I have wished to see you! When did you come? How well you remembered my habits to know where to find me. My dear John, how glad I am to see you!'

'You are the same as when I left, and this room is the same, too.'

'Yes,' she answered, 'the same, only I have had some new prints hung up—prints of fruits and leaves and birdnests. It was only done last week. When people choose pictures and poems for children they choose out such domestic ones. I would not have any of the kind; children are such undomestic animals. But, John, I am so glad to see you in this old schoolhouse again. So little has changed with us here. Some have died and some have been married,

13. NY: . . . center . . . .
16. NY: [New paragraph begins here.]
20. L, NY: . . . see you.
22. L, NY: . . . see you.'

79

and we are all a little older and the trees a little taller.'

'I have come to tell you I am going to be married.'

She became in a moment perfectly white, and sat down as though attacked with faintness. Her hand on the edge of the chair trembled.

Sherman looked at her, and went on in a bewildered, mechanical way: 'My betrothed is a Miss Leland. She has a good deal of money. You know my mother always wished me to marry some one with money. Her father, when alive, was an old client of Sherman and Saunders. She is much admired in society.' Gradually his voice became a mere murmur. He did not seem to know that he was speaking. He stopped entirely. He was looking at Mary Carton.

Everything around him was as it had been some three years before. The table was covered with cups and the floor with crumbs. Perhaps the mouse pulling at a crumb under the table was the same mouse as on that other evening. The only difference was the brooding daylight of summer and the ceaseless chirruping of the sparrows in the ivy outside. He had a confused sense of having lost his way. It was just the same feeling he had known as a child, when one dark night he had taken a wrong turning, and instead of arriving at his own house, found himself at a landmark he knew was miles from home.

A moment earlier, however difficult his life, the issues were always definite; now suddenly had entered the obscurity of another's interest.

Before this it had not occurred to him that Mary Carton had any stronger feeling for him than warm friendship.

He began again, speaking in the same mechanical way: 'Miss Leland lives with her mother near us. She is very well educated and very well connected, though she has lived always among business people.'

Miss Carton, with a great effort, had recovered her composure.

'I congratulate you,' she said. 'I hope you will be always

7. L: . . . way—'My . . . .      31. L: . . . way—'Miss . . . .
9. NY: . . . someone . . . .

80

happy. You came here on some business for your firm, I suppose? I believe they have some connection with the town still.'

'I only came here to tell you I was going to be married.'

'Do you not think it would have been better to have written?' she said, beginning to put away the children's tea-things in a cupboard by the fireplace.

'It would have been better,' he answered, drooping his head.

Without a word, locking the door behind them, they went out. Without a word they walked the grey streets. Now and then a woman or a child curtseyed as they passed. Some wondered, perhaps, to see these old friends so silent. At the rectory they bade each other good-bye.

'I hope you will be always happy,' she said. 'I will pray for you and your wife. I am very busy with the children and the old people, but I shall always find a moment to wish you well in. Good-bye now.'

They parted; the gate in the wall closed behind her. He stayed for a few moments looking up at the tops of the trees and bushes showing over the wall, and at the house a little way beyond. He stood considering his problem—her life, his life. His, at any rate, would have incident and change; hers would be the narrow existence of a woman who, failing to fulfil the only abiding wish she has ever formed, seeks to lose herself in routine—mournfulest of things on this old planet.

This had been revealed: he loved Mary Carton, she loved him. He remembered Margaret Leland, and murmured she did well to be jealous. Then all her contemptuous words about the town and its inhabitants came into his mind. Once they made no impression on him, but now the sense of personal identity having been disturbed by this sudden revelation, alien as they were to his way of thinking,

11. NY: . . . gray . . . .
12. NY: . . . courtesied . . . .
14. NY: . . . good-by.
17. L, NY: . . . and old . . . .
18. NY: Good-by . . . .
25. NY: . . . fulfill . . . .
29. NY: [New paragraph begins here.]

81

they began to press in on him. Mary, too, would have agreed with them, he thought; and might it be that at some distant time weary monotony in abandonment would have so weighed down the spirit of Mary Carton that she would be merely one of the old and sleepy whose dulness filled the place like a cloud?

He went sadly towards the hotel; everything about him, the road, the sky, the feet wherewith he walked seeming phantasmal and without meaning.

He told the waiter he would leave by the first train in the morning. 'What! and you only just come home?' the man answered. He ordered coffee and could not drink it. He went out and came in again immediately. He went down into the kitchen and talked to the servants. They told him of everything that had happened since he had gone. He was not interested, and went up to his room. 'I must go home and do what people expect of me; one must be careful to do that.'

Through all the journey home his problem troubled him. He saw the figure of Mary Carton perpetually passing through a round of monotonous duties. He saw his own life among aliens going on endlessly, wearily.

From Holyhead to London his fellow-travellers were a lady and her three young daughters, the eldest about twelve. The smooth faces shining with well-being became to him ominous symbols. He hated them. They were symbolic of the indifferent world about to absorb him, and of the vague something that was dragging him inch by inch from the nook he had made for himself in the chimney-corner. He was at one of those dangerous moments when the sense of personal identity is shaken, when one's past and present seem about to dissolve partnership. He sought refuge in memory, and counted over every word of Mary's he could remember. He forgot the present and the future.

---

4. L, NY: . . . Carton, that . . .    7. NY: . . . toward . . . .
5. NY: . . . dullness . . . .    29. L, NY: . . . chimney corner.

82

'Without love,' he said to himself, 'we would be either gods or vegetables.'

The rain beat on the window of the carriage. He began to listen; thought and memory became a blank; his mind was full of the sound of rain-drops.

# THE REV. WILLIAM HOWARD

## I

After his return to London Sherman for a time kept to himself, going straight home from his office, moody and self-absorbed, trying not to consider his problem—her life, his life. He often repeated to himself, 'I must do what people expect of me. It does not rest with me now—my choosing time is over.' He felt that whatever way he turned he would do a great evil to himself and others. To his nature all sudden decisions were difficult, and so he kept to the groove he had entered upon. It did not even occur to him to do otherwise. He never thought of breaking this engagement off and letting people say what they would. He was bound in hopelessly by a chain of congratulations.

A week passed slowly as a month. The wheels of the cabs and carriages seemed to be rolling through his mind. He often remembered the quiet river at the end of his garden in the town of Ballah. How the weeds swayed there, and the salmon leaped! At the week's end came a note from Miss Leland, complaining of his neglecting her so many days. He sent a rather formal answer, promising to call soon. To add to his other troubles, a cold east wind

6. NY: . . . that, whatever way   20. L, NY: . . . troubles a . . . .
he turned, he . . . .

arose and made him shiver continually.

One evening he and his mother were sitting silent, the one knitting, the other half-asleep. He had been writing letters and was now in a reverie. Round the walls were one or two drawings, done by him at school. His mother had got them framed. His eyes were fixed on a drawing of a stream and some astonishing cows.

A few days ago he had found an old sketchbook for children among some forgotten papers, which taught how to draw a horse by making three ovals for the basis of his body, one lying down in the middle, two standing up at each end for flank and chest, and how to draw a cow by basing its body on a square. He kept trying to fit squares into the cows. He was half inclined to take them out of their frames and retouch them on this new principle. Then he began somehow to remember the child with the swollen face who threw a stone at the dog the day he resolved to leave home first. Then some other image came. His problem moved before him in a disjointed way. He was dropping asleep. Through his reverie came the click, click of his mother's needles. She had found some London children to knit for. He was at that marchland between waking and dreaming where our thoughts begin to have a life of their own—the region where art is nurtured and inspiration born.

He started, hearing something sliding and rustling, and looked up to see a piece of cardboard fall from one end of the mantelpiece, and, driven by a slight gust of air, circle into the ashes under the grate.

'Oh,' said his mother, 'that is the portrait of the *locum tenens*.' She still spoke of the Rev. William Howard by the name she had first known him by. 'He is always being photographed. They are all over the house, and I, an old woman, have not had one taken all my life. Take it out with the tongs.' Her son, after some poking in the ashes, for it had fallen far back, brought out a somewhat dusty

5. NY: . . . drawings done . . . .     28. L: . . . mantelpiece.
8. L: . . . sketch-book . . . .     35. L, NY: . . . son after . . . .

photograph. 'That,' she continued, 'is one he sent us two or three months ago. It has been lying in the letter-rack since.'

'He is not so spick-and-span looking as usual,' said Sherman, rubbing the ashes off the photograph with his sleeve.

'By the by,' his mother replied, 'he has lost his parish, I hear. He is very mediaeval, you know, and he lately preached a sermon to prove that children who die unbaptized are lost. He had been reading up the subject and was full of it. The mothers turned against him, not being so familiar with St. Augustine as he was. There were other reasons in plenty too. I wonder that anyone can stand that monkeyish fantastic family.'

As the way is with so many country-bred people, the world for her was divided up into families rather than individuals.

While she was talking, Sherman, who had returned to his chair, leant over the table and began to write hurriedly. She was continuing her denunciation when he interrupted with: 'Mother, I have just written this letter to him:—

' "MY DEAR HOWARD:
' "Will you come and spend the autumn with us? I hear you are unoccupied just now. I am engaged to be married, as you know; it will be a long engagement. You will like my betrothed. I hope you will be great friends.
' "Yours expectantly,
' "JOHN SHERMAN." '

'You rather take me aback,' she said.

'I really like him,' he answered. 'You were always prejudiced against the Howards. Forgive me, but I really want very much to have him here.'

'Well, if you like him, I suppose I have no objection.'

'I do like him. He is very clever,' said her son, 'and

4. L, NY: . . . spick and span . . . .
6. NY: 'By the bye,' . . . .
12. L: . . . any one . . . .
17. NY: . . . talking Sherman . . . .
20. L: . . . with—'Mother . . .
21. NY: . . . him: [paragraph break] ' "MY . . . .

86

knows a great deal. I wonder he does not marry. Do you not think he would make a good husband?—for you must admit he is sympathetic.'

'It is not difficult to sympathize with everyone if you have no true principles and convictions.'

Principles and convictions were her names for that strenuous consistency attained without trouble by men and women of few ideas.

'I am sure you will like him better,' said the other, 'when you see more of him.'

'Is that photograph quite spoilt?' she answered.

'No; there was nothing on it but ashes.'

'That is a pity, for one less would be something.'

After this they both became silent, she knitting, he gazing at the cows browsing at the edge of their stream, and trying to fit squares into their bodies; but now a smile played about his lips.

Mrs. Sherman looked a little troubled. She would not object to any visitor of her son's, but quite made up her mind in no manner to put herself out to entertain the Rev. William Howard. She was puzzled as well. She did not understand the suddenness of this invitation. They usually talked over things for weeks.

## II

Next day his fellow-clerks noticed a decided improvement in Sherman's spirits. He had a lark-like cheerfulness and alacrity breaking out at odd moments. When evening came he called, for the first time since his return, on Miss Leland. She scolded him for having answered her note in such a formal way, but was sincerely glad to see him return to his allegiance. We have said he had sometimes, though rarely, a talkative fit. He had one this evening. The last play they had been to, the last party, the picture of the year, all in turn he glanced at. She was delighted. Her training had

28. L, NY: . . . him roundly for . . . .

not been in vain. Her barbarian was learning to chatter. This flattered her a deal.

'I was never engaged,' she thought, 'to a more interesting creature.'

When he had risen to go, Sherman said: 'I have a friend coming to visit me in a few days; you will suit each other delightfully. He is very mediaeval.'

'Do tell me about him; I like everything mediaeval.'

'Oh,' he cried, with a laugh, 'his mediaevalism is not in your line. He is neither a gay troubadour nor a wicked knight. He is a High Church curate.'

'Do not tell me anything more about him,' she answered; 'I will try to be civil to him, but you know I never liked curates. I have been an agnostic for many years. You, I believe, are orthodox.'

As Sherman was on his way home he met a fellow-clerk, and stopped him with: 'Are you an agnostic?'

'No. Why, what is that?'

'Oh, nothing! Good-bye,' he made answer, and hurried on his way.

## III

The letter reached the Rev. William Howard at the right moment, arriving as it did in the midst of a crisis in his fortunes. In the course of a short life he had lost many parishes. He considered himself a martyr, but was considered by his enemies a clerical coxcomb. He had a habit of getting his mind possessed with some strange opinion, or what seemed so to his parishioners, and of preaching it while the notion lasted in the most startling way. The sermon on unbaptized children was an instance. It was not so much that he thought it true as that it possessed him for a day. It was not so much the thought as his own relation to it that allured him. Then, too, he loved what appeared

5. *L, NY*: . . . go Sherman said—     *L, NY*: [New paragraph be-
'I . . . .     gins here.]
17. *L*: . . . with—'Are . . . .     19. NY: Good-by,' . . . .

88

to his parishioners to be the most unusual and dangerous practices. He put candles on the altar and crosses in unexpected places. He delighted in the intricacies of High Church costume, and was known to recommend confession and prayers for the dead.

Gradually the anger of his parishioners would increase. The rector, the washerwoman, the labourers, the squire, the doctor, the schoolteachers, the shoemakers, the butchers, the seamstresses, the local journalist, the master of the hounds, the innkeeper, the veterinary surgeon, the magistrate, the children making mud pies, all would be filled with one dread—popery. Then he would fly for consolation to his little circle of the faithful, the younger ladies, who still repeated his fine sentiments and saw him in their imaginations standing perpetually before a wall covered with tapestry and holding a crucifix in some constrained and ancient attitude. At last he would have to go, feeling for his parishioners a gay and lofty disdain, and for himself that reverent approbation one gives to the captains who lead the crusade of ideas against those who merely sleep and eat. An efficient crusader he certainly was—too efficient, indeed, for his efficiency gave to all his thoughts a certain over-completeness and isolation, and a kind of hardness to his mind. His intellect was like a musician's instrument with no sounding-board. He could think carefully and cleverly, and even with originality, but never in such a way as to make his thoughts an allusion to something deeper than themselves. In this he was the reverse of poetical, for poetry is essentially a touch from behind a curtain.[8]

This conformation of his mind helped to lead him into all manner of needless contests and to the loss of this last parish among much else. Did not the world exist for the sake of these hard, crystalline thoughts, with which he played as with so many bone spilikins, delighting in his

7. NY: . . . laborers, . . .
8. L: . . . school teachers . . . .
   NY: . . . school-teach-
   ers . . . .

19. L, NY: . . . reverend . . . .
27. CW: . . . illusion . . . .
34. L, NY: . . . *spilikins*, . . . .

own skill? and were not all who disliked them merely—the many?

In this way it came about that Sherman's letter reached Howard at the right moment. Now, next to a new parish, he loved a new friend. A visit to London meant many. He had found he was, on the whole, a success at the beginning of friendships.

He at once wrote an acceptance in his small and beautiful handwriting, and arrived shortly after his letter. Sherman, on receiving him, glanced at his neat and shining boots, the little medal at the watch-chain and the well-brushed hat, and nodded as though in answer to an inner query. He smiled approval at the slight elegant figure in its black clothes, at the satiny hair, and at the face, mobile as moving waters.

For several days the Shermans saw little of their guest. He had friends everywhere to turn into enemies and acquaintances to turn into friends. His days passed in visiting, visiting, visiting. Then there were theatres and churches to see, and new clothes to be bought, over which he was as anxious as a woman. Finally he settled down.

He passed his mornings in the smoking-room. He asked Sherman's leave to hang on the walls one or two religious pictures, without which he was not happy, and to place over the mantelpiece, under the pipe-rack, an ebony crucifix. In one corner of the room he laid a rug neatly folded for covering his knees on chilly days, and on the table a small collection of favourite books—a curious and carefully-chosen collection, in which Cardinal Newman and Bourget, St. Chrysostom and Flaubert lived together in perfect friendship.

Early in his visit Sherman brought him to the Lelands. He was a success. The three—Margaret, Sherman, and Howard—played tennis in the Square. Howard was a good

90

player, and seemed to admire Margaret. On the way home Sherman once or twice laughed to himself. It was like the clucking of a hen with a brood of chickens. He told Howard, too, how wealthy Margaret was said to be.

After this Howard always joined Sherman and Margaret at the tennis. Sometimes, too, after a little, on days when the study seemed dull and lonely, and the unfinished essay on St. Chrysostom more than usually laborious, he would saunter towards the Square before his friend's arrival, to find Margaret now alone, now with an acquaintance or two. About this time also press of work, an unusual thing with him, began to delay Sherman in town half-an-hour after his usual time. In the evenings they often talked of Margaret—Sherman frankly and carefully, as though in all anxiety to describe her as she was; and Howard with some enthusiasm: 'She has a religious vocation,' he said once, with a slight sigh.

Sometimes they played chess—a game that Sherman had recently become devoted to, for he found it drew him out of himself more than anything else.

Howard now began to notice a curious thing. Sherman grew shabbier and shabbier, and at the same time more and more cheerful. This puzzled him, for he had noticed that he himself was not cheerful when shabby, and did not even feel upright and clever when his hat was getting old. He also noticed that when Sherman was talking to him he seemed to be keeping some thought to himself. When he first came to know him long ago in Ballah he had noticed occasionally the same thing, and set it down to a kind of suspiciousness and over-caution, natural to one who lived in such an out-of-the-way place. It seemed more persistent now, however. 'He is not well-trained,' he thought; 'he is half a peasant. He has not the brilliant candour of the man of the world.'

All this while the mind of Sherman was clucking continually over its brood of thoughts. Ballah was being constantly suggested to him. The grey corner of a cloud slant-

10. NY: . . . Margaret, now . . . .    32. L: . . . well trained, . . . .
12. L, NY: . . . half an                 33. NY: . . . candor . . . .
    hour . . . .                          37. NY: . . . gray . . . .

ing its rain upon Cheapside called to mind by some remote suggestion the clouds rushing and falling in cloven surf on the seaward steep of a mountain north of Ballah. A certain street-corner made him remember an angle of the Ballah fish-market. At night a lantern, marking where the road was fenced off for mending, made him think of a tinker's cart, with its swing-can of burning coals, that used to stop on market days at the corner of Peter's Lane at Ballah. Delayed by a crush in the Strand, he heard a faint trickling of water near by; it came from a shop window where a little water-jet balanced a wooden ball upon its point. The sound suggested a cataract with a long Gaelic name, that leaped crying into the Gate of the Winds at Ballah.[9] Wandering among these memories a footstep went to and fro continually, and the figure of Mary Carton moved among them like a phantom. He was set dreaming a whole day by walking down one Sunday morning to the border of the Thames—a few hundred yards from his house—and looking at the osier-covered Chiswick eyot. It made him remember an old day-dream of his. The source of the river that passed his garden at home was a certain wood-bordered and islanded lake, whither in childhood he had often gone blackberry-gathering. At the further end was a little islet called Innisfree. Its rocky centre, covered with many bushes, rose some forty feet above the lake. Often when life and its difficulties had seemed to him like the lessons of some elder boy given to a younger by mistake, it had seemed good to dream of going away to that islet and building a wooden hut there and burning a few years out, rowing to and fro, fishing, or lying on the island slopes by day, and listening at night to the ripple of the water and the quivering of the bushes—full always of unknown creatures—and going out at morning to see the island's edge marked by the feet of birds.

These pictures became so vivid to him that the world about him—that Howard, Margaret, his mother even—be-

4. *L, NY:* . . . street corner . . . .
7. *L, NY:* . . . swing can . . . .
14. *L:* . . . continually and . . . .

24. *L, NY:* . . . called Inniscrew-in.
24. NY: . . . center, . . . .

92

gan to seem far off. He hardly seemed aware of anything they were thinking and feeling. The light that dazzled him flowed from the vague and refracting regions of hope and memory; the light that made Howard's feet unsteady was ever the too-glaring lustre of life itself.

<h1 style="text-align:center">IV</h1>

On the evening of the 20th of June, after the blinds had been pulled down and the gas lighted, Sherman was playing chess in the smoking-room, right hand against left. Howard had gone out with a message to the Lelands. He would often say, 'Is there any message I can deliver for you? I know how lazy you are, and will save you the trouble.' A message was always found for him. A pile of books lent for Sherman's improvement went home one by one.

'Look here,' said Howard's voice in the doorway, 'I have been watching you for some time. You are cheating the red men most villainously. You are forcing them to make mistakes that the white men may win. Why, a few such games would ruin any man's moral nature.'

He was leaning against the doorway, looking, to Sherman's not too critical eyes, an embodiment of all that was self-possessed and brilliant. The great care with which he dressed and his whole manner seemed to say: 'Look at me; do I not combine perfectly the zealot with the man of the world?' He seemed excited to-night. He had been talking at the Lelands, and talking well, and felt that elation which brings us many thoughts.

'My dear Sherman,' he went on, 'do cease that game. It is very bad for you. There is nobody alive who is honest enough to play a game of chess fairly out—right hand against left. We are so radically dishonest that we even cheat ourselves. We can no more play chess than we can think altogether by ourselves with security. You had much better play with me.'

5. L: . . . too glaring . . . .    22. L, NY: . . . say, 'Look . . . .
   NY: . . . too glaring lus-       25. NY: . . . Lelands', . . . .
   ter . . . .

'Very well, but you will beat me; I have not much practice,' replied the other.

They reset the men and began to play. Sherman relied most upon his bishops and queen. Howard was fondest of the knights. At first Sherman was the attacking party, but in his characteristic desire to scheme out his game many moves ahead, kept making slips, and at last had to give up, with his men nearly all gone and his king hopelessly cornered. Howard seemed to let nothing escape him. When the game was finished he leant back in his chair and said, as he rolled a cigarette: 'You do not play well.' It gave him satisfaction to feel his proficiency in many small arts. 'You do not do any of these things at all well,' he went on, with an insolence peculiar to him when excited. 'You have been really very badly brought up and stupidly educated in that intolerable Ballah. They do not understand there any, even the least, of the arts of life; they only believe in information. Men who are compelled to move in the great world, and who are also cultivated, only value the personal acquirements—self-possession, adaptability, how to dress well, how even to play tennis decently—you would not be so bad at that, by the by, if you practised—or how to paint or write effectively. They know that it is better to smoke one's cigarette with a certain charm of gesture than to have by heart all the encyclopedias. I say this not merely as a man of the world, but as a teacher of religion. A man when he rises from the grave will take with him only the things that he is in himself. He will leave behind the things that he merely possesses, learning and information not less than money and high estate. They will stay behind with his house and his clothes and his body. A collection of facts will no more help him than a collection of stamps. The learned will not get into heaven as readily as the flute-player, or even as the man who smokes a cigarette gracefully.[10] Now, you are not learned, but you have been brought up almost as badly as if you were. In that wretched

11. L: . . . a cigarette—. . .
11. L, NY: [New paragraph begins here.]
13. L: . . . on with . . . .

22. NY: . . . the bye, if you practiced—. . . .
35. L, NY: Now you . . . .

94

town they told you that education was to know that Russia is bounded on the north by the Arctic Sea, and on the west by the Baltic Ocean, and that Vienna is situated on the Danube, and that William the Third came to the throne in the year 1688. They have never taught you any personal art. Even chess-playing might have helped you at the day of judgment.'

'I am really not a worse chess-player than you. I am only more careless.'

There was a slight resentment in Sherman's voice. The other noticed it, and said, changing his manner from the insolent air of a young beauty to a self-depreciatory one, which was wont to give him at times a very genuine charm: 'It is really a great pity, for you Shermans are a deep people, much deeper than we Howards. We are like moths or butterflies, or rather rapid rivulets, while you and yours are deep pools in the forest where the beasts go to drink. No! I have a better metaphor. Your mind and mine are two arrows. Yours has got no feathers, and mine has no metal on the point. I don't know which is most needed for right conduct. I wonder where we are going to strike earth. I suppose it will be all right some day when the world has gone by and they have collected all the arrows into one quiver.'

He went over to the mantelpiece to hunt for a match, as his cigarette had gone out. Sherman had lifted a corner of the blind and was gazing over the roofs shining from a recent shower, and thinking how on such a night as this he had sat with Mary Carton by the rectory fire listening to the rain without and talking of the future and of the training of village children.

'Have you seen Miss Leland in her last new dress from Paris?' said Howard, making one of his rapid transitions. 'It is very rich in colour, and makes her look a little pale,

13. *L:* . . . charm—. . .
14. *L, NY:* [New paragraph begins here.]
16. *L:* . . . butterflies on rather . . .

16. *NY:* . . . rather, rapid . . . .
25. *L:* . . . mantlepiece . . . .
27. *NY:* . . . roofs, shining . . .
29. *NY:* . . . fire, listening . . . .
34. *NY:* . . . color, . . .

like Saint Cecilia. She is wonderful as she stands by the piano, a silver cross round her neck. We have been talking about you. She complains to me. She says you are a little barbarous. You seem to look down on style, and sometimes —you must forgive me—even on manners, and you are quite without small talk. You must really try and be worthy of that beautiful girl, with her great soul and religious genius. She told me quite sadly, too, that you are not improving.'

'No,' said Sherman, 'I am not going forward; I am at present trying to go sideways like the crabs.'

'Be serious,' answered the other. 'She told me these things with the most sad and touching voice. She makes me her confidant, you know, in many matters, because of my wide religious experience. You must really improve yourself. You must paint or something.'

'Well, I will paint or something.'

'I am quite serious, Sherman. Try and be worthy of her, a soul as gentle as Saint Cecilia's.'

'She is very wealthy,' said Sherman. 'If she were engaged to you and not to me you might hope to die a bishop.'

Howard looked at him in a mystified way and the conversation dropped. Presently Howard got up and went to his room, and Sherman, resetting the chess-board, began to play again, and, letting longer and longer pauses of reverie come between his moves, played far into the morning, cheating now in favour of the red men, now in favour of the white.

## V

The next afternoon Howard found Miss Leland sitting, reading in an alcove in her drawing-room, between a stuffed

1. *L, NY:* . . . like St. Cecilia.
4. *L, NY:* . . . barbarous; you . . . .
6. NY: . . . small-talk.
16. NY: . . . paint, or . . . .

19. *L, NY:* . . . as St. Cecilia's.
28. NY: . . . favor . . .
28. *L:* . . . men now . . .
28. NY: . . . favor . . . .
30. NY: . . . sitting reading . . .

parroquet and a blue De Morgan jar. As he was shown in he noticed, with a momentary shock, that her features were quite commonplace. Then she saw him, and at once seemed to vanish wrapped in an exulting flame of life. She stood up, flinging the book on to the seat with some violence.

'I have been reading the "Imitation of Christ," and was just feeling that I should have to become a theosophist or a socialist, or go and join the Catholic Church, or do something. How delightful it is to see you again! How is my savage getting on? It is so good of you to try and help me to reform him.'

They talked on about Sherman, and Howard did his best to console her for his shortcomings. Time would certainly improve her savage. Several times she gazed at him with those large dark eyes of hers, of which the pupils to-day seemed larger than usual. They made him feel dizzy and clutch tightly the arm of his chair. Then she began to talk about her life since childhood—how they got to the subject he never knew—and made a number of those confidences which are so dangerous because so flattering. To love—there is nothing else worth living for; but then men are so shallow. She had never found a nature deep as her own. She would not pretend that she had not often been in love, but never had any heart rung back to her the true note. As she spoke her face quivered with excitement. The exulting flame of life seemed spreading from her to the other things in the room. To Howard's eyes it seemed as though the bright pots and stuffed birds and plush curtains began to glow with a light not of this world—to glimmer like the strange and chaotic colours the mystic Blake imagined upon the scaled serpent of Eden.[11] The light seemed gradually to dim his past and future, and to make pale his good resolves. Was it not in itself that which all men are seeking, and for which all else exists?

He leant forward and took her hand, timidly and doubt-

---

1. *L:* . . . paroquet . . . .
4. *NY:* . . . vanish,
   wrapped . . . .

7. *L, NY:* . . . reading that sweet
   'Imitation . . . .
31. *NY:* . . . colors . . . .

ingly. She did not draw it away. He leant nearer and kissed her on the forehead. She gave a joyful cry, and, casting her arms round his neck, burst out, 'Ah! you—and I. We were made for each other. I hate Sherman. He is an egotist. He is a beast. He is selfish and foolish.' Releasing one of her arms she struck the seat with her hand, excitedly, and went on, 'How angry he will be! But it serves him right! How badly he is dressing. He does not know anything about anything. But you—you—I knew you were meant for me the moment I saw you.'

That evening Howard flung himself into a chair in the empty smoking-room. He lighted a cigarette; it went out. Again he lighted it; again it went out. 'I am a traitor—and that good, stupid fellow, Sherman, never to be jealous!' he thought. 'But then, how could I help it? And, besides, it cannot be a bad action to save her from a man she is so much above in refinement and feeling.' He was getting into good-humour with himself. He got up and went over and looked at the photograph of Raphael's Madonna, which he had hung over the mantelpiece. 'How like Margaret's are her big eyes!'

## VI

The next day when Sherman came home from his office he saw an envelope lying on the smoking-room table. It contained a letter from Howard, saying that he had gone away, and that he hoped Sherman would forgive his treachery, but that he was hopelessly in love with Miss Leland, and that she returned his love.

Sherman went downstairs. His mother was helping the servant to set the table.

'You will never guess what has happened.' he said. 'My

6. NY: . . . arms, she . . .
6. NY: . . . hand excitedly . . . .
15. NY: . . . help it.
18. NY: . . . good-humor . . . .
20. L: . . . mantlepiece.
22. NY: . . . day, when . . .
22. NY: . . . office, he . . . .
25. NY: . . . away and . . . .

98

affair with Margaret is over.'

'I cannot pretend to be sorry, John,' she replied. She had long considered Miss Leland among accepted things, like the chimney-pots on the roof, and submitted, as we do, to any unalterable fact, but had never praised her or expressed liking in any way. 'She puts belladonna in her eyes, and is a vixen and a flirt, and I dare say her wealth is all talk. But how did it happen?'

Her son was, however, too excited to listen.

He went upstairs and wrote the following note:

'MY DEAR MARGARET:

'I congratulate you on a new conquest. There is no end to your victories. As for me, I bow myself out with many sincere wishes for your happiness, and remain,

'Your friend,<br>'JOHN SHERMAN.'

Having posted this letter he sat down with Howard's note spread out before him, and wondered whether there was anything mean and small-minded in neatness—he himself was somewhat untidy. He had often thought so before, for their strong friendship was founded in a great measure on mutual contempt, but now immediately added, being in good-humour with the world, 'He is much cleverer than I am. He must have been very industrious at school.'

A week went by. He made up his mind to put an end to his London life. He broke to his mother his resolve to return to Ballah. She was delighted, and at once began to pack. Her old home had long seemed to her a kind of lost Eden, wherewith she was accustomed to contrast the present. When, in time, this present had grown into the past it became an Eden in turn. She was always ready for a change, if the change came to her in the form of a return to something old. Others place their ideals in the future; she laid hers in the past.

6. NY: . . . eyes and . . . .        23. NY: . . . good-humor . . . .
10. L: . . . note—. . . .

99

The only one this momentous resolution seemed to surprise was the old and deaf servant. She waited with ever-growing impatience. She would sit by the hour woolgathering on the corner of a chair with a look of bewildered delight. As the hour of departure came near she sang continually in a cracked voice.

Sherman, a few days before leaving, was returning for the last time from his office when he saw, to his surprise, Howard and Miss Leland carrying each a brown-paper bundle. He nodded good-humouredly, meaning to pass on.

'John,' she said, 'look at this brooch William gave me —a ladder leaning against the moon and a butterfly climbing up it.[12] Is it not sweet? We are going to visit the poor.'

'And I,' he said, 'am going to catch eels. I am leaving town.'

He made his excuses, saying he had no time to wait, and hurried off. She looked after him with a mournful glance, strange in anybody who had exchanged one lover for another more favoured.

'Poor fellow,' murmured Howard, 'he is brokenhearted.'

'Nonsense,' answered Miss Leland, somewhat snappishly.

1. *NY:* [No paragraph break.]    10. *NY:* . . . good-humoredly,
3. *NY:* . . . ever growing . . . .    . . . .
9. *L:* . . . brown paper . . . .    19. *NY:* . . . favored.

# JOHN SHERMAN RETURNS TO BALLAH

## I

This being the homeward trip, S.S. *Lavinia* carried no cattle, but many passengers. As the sea was smooth and the voyage near its end, they lounged about the deck in groups. Two cattle-merchants were leaning over the taffrail smoking. In appearance they were something between betting-men and commercial travellers. For years they had done all their sleeping in steamers and trains. A short distance from them a clerk from Liverpool, with a consumptive cough, walked to and fro, a little child holding his hand. Shortly he would be landed in a boat putting off from the shore for the purpose. He had come hoping that his native air of Teeling Head would restore him. The little child was a strange contrast—her cheeks ruddy with perfect health. Further forward, talking to one of the crew, was a man with a red face and slightly unsteady step. In the companion-house was a governess, past her first youth, very much afraid of sea-sickness. She had brought her luggage up and heaped it round her to be ready for landing. Sherman sat on a pile of cable looking out over the sea. It was just noon;

4. L, NY: . . . cattle merchants . . . .
5. L, NY: . . . betting

15. L: . . . companion house . . .
17. NY: . . . seasickness.

men . . . .

S.S. *Lavinia,* having passed by Tory and Rathlin, was approaching the Donegal cliffs. They were covered by a faint mist, which made them loom even vaster than they were. To westward the sun shone on a perfectly blue sea. Seagulls came out of the mist and plunged into the sunlight, and out of the sunlight and plunged into the mist. To the westward gannets were striking continually, and a porpoise showed now and then, his fin and back gleaming in the sun. Sherman was more perfectly happy than he had been for many a day, and more ardently thinking. All nature seemed full of a Divine fulfilment. Everything fulfilled its law—fulfilment that is peace, whether it be for good or for evil, for evil also has its peace, the peace of the birds of prey. Sherman looked from the sea to the ship and grew sad. Upon this thing, crawling slowly along the sea, moved to and fro many mournful and slouching figures. He looked from the ship to himself and his eyes filled with tears. On himself, on these moving figures, hope and memory fed like flames.

Again his eyes gladdened, for he knew he had found his present. He would live in his love and the day as it passed. He would live that his law might be fulfilled. Now, was he sure of this truth—the saints on the one hand, the animals on the other, live in the moment as it passes. Thitherward had his days brought him. This was the one grain they had ground. To grind one grain is sufficient for a lifetime.[13]

## II

A few days later Sherman was hurrying through the town of Ballah. It was Saturday, and he passed down through the marketing country people, and the old women with baskets of cakes and gooseberries and long pieces of sugarstick shaped like walking-sticks, and called by children 'Peggie's leg.'

11. NY: . . . fulfillment.
11. NY: . . . fulfillment . . . .
23. L, NY: . . . truth?—. . . .

29. NY: . . . country-
    people, . . . .
31. NY: . . . walking sticks, . . . .

Now, as two months earlier, he was occasionally recognized and greeted, and, as before, went on without knowing, his eyes full of unintelligent sadness because the mind was making merry afar. They had the look we see in the eyes of animals and dreamers. Everything had grown simple, his problem had taken itself away. He was thinking what he would say to Mary Carton. Now they would be married, they would live in a small house with a green door and a new thatch, and a row of beehives under a hedge. He knew where just such a house stood empty. The day before he and his mother had discussed, with their host of the Imperial Hotel, this question of houses. They knew the peculiarities of every house in the neighbourhood, except two or three built while they were away. All day Sherman and his mother had gone over the merits of the few they were told were empty. She wondered why her son had grown so unpractical. Once he was so easily pleased—the row of beehives and the new thatch did not for her settle the question. She set it all down to Miss Leland and the plays, and the singing, and the belladonna, and remembered with pleasure how many miles of uneasy water lay between the town of Ballah and these things.

She did not know what else besides the row of beehives and the new thatch her son's mind ran on as he walked among the marketing country people, and the gooseberry sellers, and the merchants of 'Peggie's leg,' and the boys playing marbles in odd corners, and the men in waistcoats with flannel sleeves driving carts, and the women driving donkeys with creels of turf or churns of milk. Just now she was trying to remember whether she used to buy her wool for knitting at Miss Peter's or from Mrs. Macallough's at the bridge. One or other sold it a halfpenny a skein cheaper. She never knew what went on inside her son's

---

1. L: . . . earlier he . . . .          25. NY: . . . country-people,
13. NY: . . . neighborhood . . . .          . . .
19. NY: . . . Leland, and . . . .          25. NY: . . . gooseberry-sellers,
23. L, CW: . . . beside . . .          . . . .

mind, she had always her own fish to fry. Blessed are the unsympathetic. They preserve their characters in an iron bottle while the most of us poor mortals are going about the planet vainly searching for any kind of a shell to contain us, and evaporating the while.

Sherman began to mount the hill to the vicarage. He was happy. Because he was happy he began to run. Soon the steepness of the hill made him walk. He thought about his love for Mary Carton. Seen by the light of this love everything that had happened to him was plain now. He had found his centre of unity. His childhood had prepared him for this love. He had been solitary, fond of favourite corners of fields, fond of going about alone, unhuman like the birds and the leaves, his heart empty. How clearly he remembered his first meeting with Mary. They were both children. At a school treat they watched the fire-balloon ascend, and followed it a little way over the fields together. What friends they became, growing up together, reading the same books, thinking the same thoughts!

As he came to the door and pulled at the great hanging iron bell-handle, the fire-balloon reascended in his heart, surrounded with cheers and laughter.

## III

He kept the servant talking for a moment or two before she went for Miss Carton. The old rector, she told him, was getting less and less able to do much work. Old age had come almost suddenly upon him. He seldom moved from the fireside. He was getting more and more absent-minded. Once lately he had brought his umbrella into the reading-desk. More and more did he leave all things to his children —to Mary Carton and her younger sisters.

When the servant had gone, Sherman looked round the somewhat gloomy room. In the window hung a canary in a painted cage. Outside was a narrow piece of shaded ground between the window and the rectory wall. The laurel and holly bushes darkened the window a good deal. On a table in the centre of the room were evangelistic books with gilded covers. Round the mirror over the mantelpiece were stuck various parish announcements, thrust between the glass and the gilding. On a small side-table was a copper ear-trumpet.

How familiar everything seemed to Sherman! Only the room seemed smaller than it did three years before, and close to the table with the ear-trumpet, at one side of the fireplace before the arm-chair, was a new threadbare patch in the carpet.

Sherman recalled how in this room he and Mary Carton had sat in winter by the fire, building castles in the air for each other. So deeply meditating was he that she came in and stood unnoticed beside him.

'John,' she said at last, 'it is a great pleasure to see you so soon again. Are you doing well in London?'

'I have left London.'

'Are you married, then? You must introduce me to your wife.'

'I shall never be married to Miss Leland.'

'What?'

'She has preferred another—my friend William Howard. I have come here to tell you something, Mary.' He went and stood close to her and took her hand tenderly. 'I have always been very fond of you. Often in London, when I was trying to think of another kind of life, I used to see this fireside and you sitting beside it, where we used to sit and talk about the future. Mary—Mary,' he held her hand in both his—'you will be my wife?'

1. *L, NY:* . . . gone Sherman . . . .
6. NY: . . . center . . . .
7. *L:* . . . . mantlepiece . . . .
9. *L, NY:* . . . side table . . . .
11. *L, NY:* . . . to Sherman
14. NY: . . . armchair, . . . .

*105*

'You do not love me, John,' she answered, drawing herself away. 'You have come to me because you think it your duty. I have had nothing but duty all my life.'

'Listen,' he said. 'I was very miserable; I invited Howard to stay with us. One morning I found a note on the smoking-room table to say that Margaret had accepted him, and I have come here to ask you to marry me. I never cared for anyone else.'

He found himself speaking hurriedly, as though anxious to get the words said and done with. It now seemed to him that he had done ill in this matter of Miss Leland. He had not before thought of it—his mind had always been busy with other things. Mary Carton looked at him wonderingly.

'John,' she said at last, 'did you ask Mr. Howard to stay with you on purpose to get him to fall in love with Miss Leland, or to give you an excuse for breaking off your engagement, as you knew he flirted with everyone?'

'Margaret seems very fond of him. I think they are made for each other,' he answered.

'Did you ask him to London on purpose?'

'Well, I will tell you,' he faltered. 'I was very miserable. I had drifted into this engagement I don't know how. Margaret glitters and glitters and glitters, but she is not of my kind. I suppose I thought, like a fool, I should marry someone who was rich. I found out soon that I loved nobody but you. I got to be always thinking of you and of this town. Then I heard that Howard had lost his curacy, and asked him up. I just left them alone and did not go near Margaret much. I knew they were made for each other. Do not let us talk of them,' he continued, eagerly. 'Let us talk about the future. I will take a farm and turn farmer. I dare say my uncle will not give me anything when he dies because I have left his office. He will call me a ne'er-do-well, and say I would squander it. But you and I—we will get married, will we not? We will be very

8. L: . . . any one . . . .          32. NY: . . . daresay . . . .
17. L: . . . every one?'              33. NY: . . . dies, because . . . .
25. L: . . . some one . . . .

106

happy,' he went on, pleadingly. 'You will still have your charities, and I shall be busy with my farm. We will surround ourselves with a wall. The world will be on the outside, and on the inside we and our peaceful lives.'

'Wait,' she said; 'I will give you your answer,' and going into the next room returned with several bundles of letters. She laid them on the table; some were white and new, some slightly yellow with time.

'John,' she said, growing very pale, 'here are all the letters you ever wrote me from your earliest boyhood.' She took one of the large candles from the mantelpiece, and, lighting it, placed it on the hearth. Sherman wondered what she was going to do with it. 'I will tell you,' she went on, 'what I had thought to carry to the grave unspoken. I have loved you for a long time. When you came and told me you were going to be married to another I forgave you, for man's love is like the wind, and I prayed that God might bless you both.' She leant down over the candle, her face pale and contorted with emotion. 'All these letters after that grew very sacred. Since we were never to be married they grew a portion of my life, separated from everything and everyone—a something apart and holy. I re-read them all, and arranged them in little bundles according to their dates, and tied them with thread. Now I and you—we have nothing to do with each other any more.'

She held the bundle of letters in the flame. He got up from his seat. She motioned him away imperiously. He looked at the flame in a bewildered way. The letters fell in little burning fragments about the hearth. It was all like a terrible dream. He watched those steady fingers hold letter after letter in the candle flame, and watched the candle burning on like a passion in the grey daylight of universal existence. A draught from under the door began blowing the ash about the room. The voice said—

1. NY: . . . on pleadingly.   22. L: . . . every one . . . .
11. L: . . . mantlepiece . . . .   33. NY: . . . gray . . . .
13. NY: [New paragraph begins   35. NY: . . . voice said: . . . .
    here.]

'You tried to marry a rich girl. You did not love her, but knew she was rich. You tired of her as you tire of so many things, and behaved to her most wrongly, most wickedly and treacherously. When you were jilted you came again to me and to the idleness of this little town. We had all hoped great things of you. You seemed good and honest.'

'I loved you all along,' he cried. 'If you would marry me we would be very happy. I loved you all along,' he repeated —this helplessly, several times over. The bird shook a shower of seed on his shoulder. He picked one of them from the collar of his coat and turned it over in his fingers mechanically. 'I loved you all along.'

'You have done no duty that came to you. You have tired of everything you should cling to; and now you have come to this little town because here is idleness and irresponsibility.'

The last letter lay in ashes on the hearth. She blew out the candle, and replaced it among the photographs on the mantelpiece, and stood there as calm as a portion of the marble.

'John, our friendship is over—it has been burnt in the candle.'

He started forward, his mind full of appeals half-stifled with despair, on his lips gathered incoherent words: 'She will be happy with Howard. They were made for each other. I slipped into it. I always thought I should marry someone who was rich. I never loved anyone but you. I did not know I loved you at first. I thought about you always. You are the root of my life.'

Steps were heard outside the door at the end of a passage. Mary Carton went to the door and called. The steps turned and came nearer. With a great effort Sherman controlled himself. The door opened, and a tall, slight girl of twelve came into the room. A strong smell of garden mould rose from a basket in her hands. Sherman recog-

9. NY: . . . repeated this . . . .  27. L: . . . any one . . . .
19. L: . . . mantlepiece, . . . .  35. NY: . . . mold . . . .
27. L: . . . some one . . . .

nized the child who had given him tea that evening in the schoolhouse three years before.

'Have you finished weeding the carrots?' said Mary Carton.

'Yes, Miss.'

'Then you are to weed that small bed under the pear-tree by the tool-house. Do not go yet, child. This is Mr. Sherman. Sit down a little.'

The child sat down on the corner of a chair with a scared look in her eyes. Suddenly she said—

'Oh, what a lot of burnt paper!'

'Yes; I have been burning some old letters.'

'I think,' said John, 'I will go now.' Without a word of farewell he went out, almost groping his way.

He had lost the best of all the things he held dear. Twice he had gone through the fire. The first time worldly ambition left him; the second, love. An hour before the air had been full of singing and peace that was resonant like joy. Now he saw standing before his Eden the angel with the flaming sword. All the hope he had ever gathered about him had taken itself off, and the naked soul shivered.

## IV

The road under his feet felt gritty and barren. He hurried away from town. It was late afternoon. Trees cast bands of shadow across the road. He walked rapidly as if pursued. About a mile to the west of the town he came on a large wood bordering the road and surrounding a deserted house. Some local rich man once lived there, now it was given over to a caretaker who lived in two rooms in the back part. Men were at work cutting down trees in two or three parts of the wood. Many places were quite bare. A mass of ruins—a covered well, and the wreckage of castle

---

6. NY: . . . the pear tree by the toolhouse.
10. NY: . . . she said: . . . .
17. L, NY: . . . him, on the second love.
24. NY: . . . rapidly, as . . . .
25. L, NY: . . . the south of . . . .
31. NY: . . . well and . . .

wall—that had been roofed with green for centuries, lifted themselves up, bare as anatomies.[14] The sight intensified, by some strange sympathy, his sorrow, and he hurried away as from a thing accursed of God.

The road lead to the foot of a mountain, topped by a cairn supposed in popular belief to be the grave of Maeve, Mab of the fairies, and considered by antiquarians to mark the place where certain prisoners were executed in legendary times as sacrifices to the moon.[15]

He began to climb the mountain. The sun was on the rim of the sea. It stayed there without moving, for as he ascended he saw an ever-widening circle of water.

He threw himself down upon the cairn. The sun sank under the sea. The Donegal headlands mixed with the surrounding blue. The stars grew out of heaven.

Sometimes he got up and walked to and fro. Hours passed. The stars, the streams down in the valley, the wind moving among the boulders, the various unknown creatures rustling in the silence—all these were contained within themselves, fulfilling their law, content to be alone, content to be with others, having the peace of God or the peace of the birds of prey. He only did not fulfil his law; something that was not he, that was not nature, that was not God, had made him and her he loved its tools. Hope, memory, tradition, conformity, had been laying waste their lives. As he thought this the night seemed to crush him with its purple foot. Hour followed hour. At midnight he started up, hearing a faint murmur of clocks striking the hour in the distant town. His face and hands were wet with tears, his clothes saturated with dew.

He turned homeward, hurriedly flying from the terrible firmament. What had this glimmering and silence to do with him—this luxurious present? He belonged to the past and the future. With pace somewhat slackened, because of the furze, he came down into the valley. Along the north-

1. L, NY: . . . centuries      12. NY: . . . ever widening . . . .
    lifted . . . .              18. NY: . . . bowlders, . . . .
                                         22. NY: . . . fulfill . . .

ern horizon moved a perpetual dawn, travelling eastward as the night advanced. Once, as he passed a marsh near a lime-kiln, a number of small birds rose chirruping from where they had been clinging among the reeds. Once, standing still for a moment where two roads crossed on a hill-side, he looked out over the dark fields. A white stone rose in the middle of a field, a score of yards in front of him. He knew the place well; it was an ancient burying-ground. He looked at the stone, and suddenly filled by the terror of the darkness children feel, began again his hurried walk.

He re-entered Ballah by the southern side. In passing he looked at the rectory. To his surprise a light burned in the drawing-room. He stood still. The dawn was brightening towards the east, but all round him was darkness, seeming the more intense to his eyes for their being fresh from the unshaded fields. In the midst of this darkness shone the lighted window. He went over to the gate and looked in. The room was empty. He was about to turn away when he noticed a white figure standing close to the gate. The latch creaked and the gate moved slowly on its hinges.

'John,' said a trembling voice, 'I have been praying, and a light has come to me. I wished you to be ambitious—to go away and do something in the world. You did badly, and my poor pride was wounded. You do not know how much I had hoped from you; but it was all pride—all pride and foolishness. You love me. I ask no more. We need each other; the rest is with God.'

She took his hand in hers, and began caressing it. 'We have been shipwrecked. Our goods have been cast into the sea.' Something in her voice told of the emotion that divides the love of woman from the love of man. She looked upon him whom she loved as full of a helplessness that needed protection, a reverberation of the feeling of the mother for the child at the breast.

6. NY: . . . hillside, . . . .
9. NY: . . . stone and, suddenly . . . .

9. L, NY: . . . by that terror . . . .
15. NY: . . . toward . . . .

# DHOYA

# I

Long ago, before the earliest stone of the Pyramids was laid, before the Bo tree of Buddha unrolled its first leaf, before a Japanese had painted on a temple wall the horse that every evening descended and trampled the rice-fields, before the ravens of Thor had eaten their first worm together, there lived a man of giant stature and of giant strength named Dhoya. One evening Fomorian galleys had entered the Bay of the Red Cataract,[16] now the Bay of Ballah, and there deserted him. Though he rushed into the water and hurled great stones after them, they were out of reach. From earliest childhood the Fomorians had held him captive and compelled him to toil at the oar, but when his strength had come his fits of passion made him a terror to all on board. Sometimes he would tear the seats of the galley from under the rowers, and drive the rowers up into the shrouds, where they would cling until the passion left him. 'The demons,' they said, 'have made him their own.'

1. [No paragraph indentation in *CW*. This lack of indentation at the beginning of a story is characteristic of *CW*.]
1. *L*, *NY*: . . . pyramids . . .
4. *NY*: . . . ricefields, . . . .
10. *L*, *NY*: . . . them they . . . .
15. *L*, *NY*: . . . gallery from their places, at others drive the rowers to some corner where, trembling, they would watch him pacing to and fro till the passion left him.

So they enticed him on shore, he having on his head a mighty stone pitcher to fill with water, and deserted him.

When the last sail had dropped over the rim of the world, he rose from where he had flung himself down on the sands and hurried through the forest eastward. After a time he reached that lake among the mountains where in later times Diarmuid drove down four stakes and made thereon a platform with four flags in the centre for a hearth, and placed over all a roof of wicker and skins, and hid his Grania, islanded thereon. Still eastward he went, what is now Bulben on one side, Cope's mountain on the other, until at last he threw himself at full length in a deep cavern and slept. Henceforward he made this cavern his lair, issuing forth to hunt the deer or the bears or the mountain oxen. Slowly the years went by, his fits of fury growing more and more frequent, though there was no one but his own shadow to rave against. When his fury was on him even the bats and the owls, and the brown frogs that crept out of the grass at twilight, would hide themselves— even the bats and the owls and the brown frogs. These he had made his friends, and let them crawl and perch about him, for at times he would be very gentle, and they too were sullen and silent—the outcasts from they knew not what. But most of all, things placid and beautiful feared him. He would watch for hours, hidden in the leaves, to reach his hand out slowly and carefully at last, and seize and crush some glittering halcyon.

Slowly the years went by and human face he never saw, but sometimes, when the gentle mood was on him and it was twilight, a presence seemed to float invisibly by him and sigh softly, and once or twice he awoke from sleep with the sensation of a finger having rested for a moment on his forehead, and would mutter a prayer to the moon that

4. L, NY: . . . world he . . .
5. L, NY: . . . paced through the forests eastward.
7. L, NY: . . . Dermot . . .
8. NY: . . . center . . . .
11. L, NY: . . . Bulban . . . .
18. L, NY: . . . brown toads that . . .

19. L: . . . twilight would . . .
20. L, NY: . . . brown toads.
33. L, NY: . . . prayer to the moon before turning to sleep again—the moon that glimmered through the door of his cave. 'O . . .

116

glimmered through the door of his cave before turning to sleep again. 'O moon,' he would say, 'that wanderest in the blue cave of the sky, more white than the beard of Partholan, whose years were five hundred, sullen and solitary, sleeping only on the floor of the sea: keep me from the evil spirits of the islands of the lake southward beyond the mountains, and the evil spirits of the caves northward beyond the mountains, and the evil spirits who wave their torches by the mouth of the river eastward beyond the valley, and the evil spirits of the pools westward beyond the mountains, and I will offer you a bear and a deer in full horn, O solitary of the cave divine, and if any have done you wrong I will avenge you.'

Gradually, however, he began to long for this mysterious touch.

At times he would make journeys into distant parts, and once the mountain bulls gathered together, proud of their overwhelming numbers and their white horns, and followed him with great bellowing westward, he being laden with their tallest, well-nigh to his cave, and would have gored him, but, pacing into a pool of the sea to his shoulders, he saw them thunder away, losing him in the darkness. The place where he stood is called Pooldhoya to this day.

So the years went slowly by, and ever deeper and deeper came his moodiness, and more often his fits of wrath. Once in his gloom he paced the forests for miles, now this way, now that, until, returning in the twilight, he found himself standing on a cliff southward of the lake that was southward of the mountains. The moon was rising. The sound of the swaying of reeds floated from beneath, and the twittering of the flocks of reed-wrens who love to cling on the moving stems. It was the hour of votaries. He turned to the moon, then hurriedly gathered a pile of leaves and branches, and making a fire cast thereon wild strawberries

2. *L, NY:* . . . wandereth . . .
3. *L, NY:* . . . cave, more . . . .
17. *L, NY:* . . . mountain oxen gathered . . . .
27. *L, NY:* . . . way now . . . .
36. *L, NY:* . . . quicken tree.

and the fruit of the quicken-tree. As the smoke floated
upwards a bar of faint purple clouds drifted over the
moon's face—a refusal of the sacrifice. Hurrying through
the surrounding woods he found an owl sleeping in the
hollow of a tree, and returning cast him on the fire. Still the
clouds gathered. Again he searched the woods. This time it
was a badger that he cast among the flames. Time after time
he came and went, sometimes returning immediately with
some live thing, at others not till the fire had almost burnt
itself out. Deer, wild swine, birds, all to no purpose. Higher
and higher he piled the burning branches, the flames and
the smoke waved and circled like the lash of a giant's whip.
Gradually the nearer islands passed the rosy colour on to
their more distant brethren. The reed-wrens of the furthest
reed beds disturbed amid their sleep must have wondered
at the red gleam reflected in each other's eyes. Useless his
night-long toil; the clouds covered the moon's face more
and more, until, when the long fire-lash was at its brightest,
they drowned her completely in a surge of unbroken mist.
Raging against the fire he scattered with his staff the burning branches, and trampled in his fury the sacrifical embers
beneath his feet. Suddenly a voice in the surrounding darkness called him softly by name. He turned. For years no
articulate voice had sounded in his ears. It seemed to rise
from the air just beneath the verge of the precipice. Holding by a hazel bush he leaned out, and for a moment it
seemed to him the form of a beautiful woman floated
faintly before him, but changed as he watched to a little
cloud of vapour; and from the nearest of the haunted
islands there came assuredly a whiff of music. Then behind
him in the forest said the voice, 'Dhoya, my beloved.' He
rushed in pursuit; something white was moving before him.
He stretched out his hand; it was only a mass of white
campion trembling in the morning breeze, for an ashen

5. NY: . . . time a badger was     15. NY: . . . others' eyes.
    uselessly cast . . . .            16. NY: . . . his nightlong toil;
12. NY: . . . color . . . .              . . .
13. NY: . . . furtherest reed-beds,   17. NY: . . . more until, . . .
    disturbed amid their sleep,       17. L, NY: . . . fire lash . . . .
    must . . .                        28. NY: . . . vapor; . . . .

morning was just touching the mists on the eastern mountains. Beginning suddenly to tremble with supernatural fear Dhoya turned homewards. Everything was changed; dark shadows seemed to come and go, and elfin chatter to pass upon the breeze. But when he reached the shelter of the pine woods all was still as of old. He slackened his speed. Those solemn pine-trees soothed him with their vast unsociability—many and yet each one alone. Once or twice, when in some glade further than usual from its kind arose a pine-tree larger than the rest, he paused with bowed head to mutter an uncouth prayer to that dark outlaw. As he neared his cave and came from the deep shade into the region of mountain-ash and hazel, the voices seemed again to come and go, and the shadows to circle round him, and once a voice said, he imagined, in accents faint and soft as falling dew, 'Dhoya, my beloved.' But a few yards from the cave all grew suddenly silent.

## II

Slower and slower he went, with his eyes on the ground, bewildered by all that was happening. A few feet from the cave he stood still, counting aimlessly the round spots of light made by the beams slanting through trees that hid with their greenness, as in the centre of the sea, that hollow rock. As over and over he counted them, he heard, first with the ear only, then with the mind also, a footstep going to and fro within the cave. Lifting his eyes he saw the same figure seen on the cliff—the figure of a woman, beautiful and young. Her dress was white, save for a border of feathers dyed the fatal red of the spirits. She had arranged in one corner the spears, and in the other the brushwood and

3. L: . . . Dhoya paced homewards.
NY: . . . Dhoya paced homeward.
7. NY: . . . pine trees . . .
8. NY: . . . many, and . . . .
9. L: . . . arose some pine-tree . . . .

NY: . . . arose some pine tree . . . .
11. L, NY: . . . . outlaw. But when issuing once more, as he neared his cave, into the region of mountain ash and hazel the voices . . . .
18. NY: Then slower and . . . .
22. NY: . . . center . . . .

branches used for the fire, and spread upon the ground the skins, and now began pulling vainly at the great stone pitcher of the Fomorians.

Suddenly she saw him and with a burst of laughter flung her arms round his neck, crying, 'Dhoya, I have left my world far off. My people—on the floor of the lake they are dancing and singing, and on the islands of the lake; always happy, always young, always without change. I have left them for thee, Dhoya, for they cannot love. Only the changing, and moody, and angry, and weary can love. I am beautiful; love me, Dhoya. Do you hear me? I left the places where they dance, Dhoya, for thee!' For long she poured out a tide of words, he answering at first little, then more and more as she melted away the silence of so many inarticulate years; and all the while she gazed on him with eyes, no ardour could rob of the mild and mysterious melancholy that watches us from the eyes of animals—sign of unhuman reveries.

Many days passed over these strangely-wedded ones. Sometimes when he asked her, 'Do you love me?' she would answer, 'I do not know, but I long for your love endlessly.' Often at twilight, returning from hunting, he would find her bending over a stream that flowed near to the cave, decking her hair with feathers and reddening her lips with the juice of a wild berry.

He was very happy secluded in that deep forest. Hearing the faint murmurs of the western sea, they seemed to have outlived change. But Change is everywhere, with the tides and the stars fastened to her wheel. Every blood-drop in their lips, every cloud in the sky, every leaf in the world changed a little, while they brushed back their hair and kissed. All things change save only the fear of change. And yet for this hour Dhoya was happy and as full of dreams as an old man or an infant—for dreams wander nearest to the grave and the cradle.

Once, as he was returning home from hunting, by the

4. *L, NY:* . . . him, and . . .  could . . . .
4. *L, NY:* . . . of wild laugh- 19. *L, NY:* . . . strangely
ter . . . .  wedded . . . .
16. *NY:* . . . eyes no ardor  29. *L:* . . . blood drop . . . .

120

northern edge of the lake, at the hour when the owls cry to each other, 'It is time to be abroad,' and the last flutter of the wind has died away, leaving under every haunted island an image legible to the least hazel branch, there suddenly stood before him a slight figure, at the edge of the narrow sand-line, dark against the glowing water. Dhoya drew nearer. It was a man leaning on his spear-staff, on his head a small red cap. His spear was slender and tipped with shining metal; the spear of Dhoya of wood, one end pointed and hardened in the fire. The red-capped stranger silently raised that slender spear and thrust at Dhoya, who parried with his pointed staff.

For a long while they fought. The last vestige of sunset passed away and the stars came out. Underneath them the feet of Dhoya beat up the ground, but the feet of the other as he rushed hither and thither, matching his agility with the mortal's mighty strength, made neither shadow nor footstep on the sands. Dhoya was wounded, and growing weary a little, when the other leaped away, and, crouching down by the water, began: 'You have carried away by some spell unknown the most beautiful of our bands—you who have neither laughter nor singing. Restore her, Dhoya, and go free.' Dhoya answered him no word, and the other rose and again thrust at him with the spear. They fought to and fro upon the sands until the dawn touched with olive the distant sky, and then his anger-fit, long absent, fell on Dhoya, and he closed with his enemy and threw him, and put his knee on his chest and his hands on his throat, and would have crushed all life out of him, when lo! he held beneath his knee no more than a bundle of reeds.

Nearing home in the early morning he heard the voice he loved, singing:

> Full moody is my love and sad,
>   His moods bow low his sombre crest,
> I hold him dearer than the glad,
>   And he shall slumber on my breast.

20. L, NY: . . . began—      32. NY: . . . loved, singing—. . .
    'You . . . .                 33. L: 'Full . . .
26. L, NY: . . . anger fit, . . . .   34. NY: . . . somber . . . .

My love hath many an evil mood,
  Ill words for all things soft and fair,
I hold him dearer than the good,
  My fingers feel his amber hair.

No tender wisdom floods the eyes
  That watch me with their suppliant light—
I hold him dearer than the wise
  And for him make me wise and bright.[17]

And when she saw him she cried, 'An old mortal song heard floating from a tent of skin, as we rode, I and mine, through a camping-place at night.' From that day she was always either singing wild and melancholy songs or else watching him with that gaze of animal reverie.

Once he asked, 'How old are you?'

'A thousand years, for I am young.'

'I am so little to you,' he went on, 'and you are so much to me—dawn, and sunset, tranquillity, and speech, and solitude.'

'Am I so much?' she said; 'say it many times!' and her eyes seemed to brighten and her breast heaved with joy.

Often he would bring her the beautiful skins of animals, and she would walk to and fro on them, laughing to feel their softness under her feet. Sometimes she would pause and ask suddenly, 'Will you weep for me when we have parted?' and he would answer, 'I will die then'; and she would go on rubbing her feet to and fro in the soft skin.

And so Dhoya grew tranquil and gentle, and Change seemed still to have forgotten them, having so much on her hands. The stars rose and set watching them smiling together, and the tides ebbed and flowed, bringing mutability to all save them. But always everything changes, save only the fear of Change.

1. L: 'My . . .
1. L, NY: . . . mood / Ill . . . .
5. L: 'No . . .
8. L: . . . bright.'
17. L: . . . tranquility, . . . .
29. NY: . . . together and . . . .

# III

One evening as they sat in the inner portion of the cave, watching through the opening the paling of the sky and the darkening of the leaves, and counting the budding stars, Dhoya suddenly saw stand before him the dark outline of him he fought on the lake sand, and heard at the same instant his companion sigh.

The stranger approached a little, and said, 'Dhoya, we have fought heretofore, and now I have come to play chess against thee, for well thou knowest, dear to the perfect warrior after war is chess.'

'I know it,' answered Dhoya.

'And when we have played, Dhoya, we will name the stake.'

'Do not play,' whispered his companion at his side.

But Dhoya, being filled with his anger-fit at the sight of his enemy, answered, 'I will play, and I know well the stake you mean, and I name this for mine, that I may again have my knee on your chest and my hands on your throat, and that you will not again change into a bundle of wet reeds.' His companion lay down on a skin and began to cry a little.

Dhoya felt sure of winning. He had often played in his boyhood, before the time of his anger-fits, with his masters of the galley; and besides, he could always return to his hands and his weapons once more.

Now the floor of the cave was of smooth, white sand, brought from the seashore in his great Fomorian pitcher, to make it soft for his beloved to walk upon; before it had been, as it now is, of rough clay. On this sand the red-capped stranger marked out with his spear-point a chess-board, and marked with rushes, crossed and recrossed each alternate square, fixing each end of the rush in the sand, until a complete board was finished of white and green squares, and then drew from a bag large chessmen of min-

15. L, NY: . . . anger fit . . . .     25. NY: . . . smooth white . . .
22. L, NY: . . . anger fits, . . . .     26. L: . . . sea-shore . . . .
                                         33. L, NY: . . . chess-men . . . .

gled wood and silver. Two or three would have made an armful for a child. Standing each at his end they began to play. The game did not last long. No matter how carefully Dhoya played, each move went against him. At last, leaping back from the board, he cried, 'I have lost!' The two spirits were standing together at the entrance. Dhoya seized his spear, but slowly the figures began to fade, first a star and then the leaves showed through their forms. Soon all had vanished away.

Then, understanding his loss, he threw himself on the ground, and rolling hither and thither, roared like a wild beast. All night long he lay on the ground, and all the next day till nightfall. He had crumbled his staff unconsciously between his fingers into small pieces, and now, full of dull rage, the pointed end of the staff still in his hand, arose and went forth westward. In a ravine of the northern mountain he came on the tracks of wild horses. Soon one passed him fearlessly, knowing nothing of man. He drove the pointed end of the staff deep in the flank, making a great wound, sending the horse rushing with short screams down the mountain. Other horses passed him one by one, driven southward by a cold wind laden with mist, arisen in the night-time. Towards the end of the ravine stood one black and huge, the leader of the herd. Dhoya leaped on his back with a loud cry that sent a raven circling from the neighbouring cliff, and the horse, after vainly seeking to throw him, rushed off towards the north-west, over the heights of the mountains where the mists floated. The moon, clear sometimes of the flying clouds, from low down in the south-east, cast a pale and mutable light, making their shadow rise before them on the mists, as though they

5. L: . . . board he . . . .
7. NY: . . . to fade—first . . . .
10. L, NY: Then, realizing his . . . .
15. L, NY: . . . rage, arose . . . .
19. L, NY: . . . of man. The pointed end of his staff he still carried. He drove it deep in the flank, . . .

19. L, NY: . . . a long wound, . . . .
21. NY: . . . him, one . . . .
23. NY: Toward . . . .
26. NY: . . . neighboring . . .
27. NY: . . . off toward the north-west, . . . .
30. NY: . . . southeast . . .

pursued some colossal demon, sombre on his black charger. Then leaving the heights they rushed down that valley where, in far later times, Diarmuid hid in a deep cavern his Grania, and passed the stream where Muadhan, their savage servant, caught fish for them on a hook baited with a quicken-berry. On over the plains, on northward, mile after mile, the wild gigantic horse leaping cliff and chasm in his terrible race; on until the mountains of what is now Donegal rose before them—over these among the clouds, driving rain blowing in their faces from the sea, Dhoya knowing not whither he went, or why he rode. On—the stones loosened by the hoofs rumbling down into the valleys—till far in the distance he saw the sea, a thousand feet below him; then, fixing his eyes thereon, and using the spear-point as a goad, he roused his black horse into redoubled speed, until horse and rider plunged headlong into the Western Sea.

Sometimes the cotters on the mountains of Donegal hear on windy nights a sudden sound of horses' hoofs, and say to each other, 'There goes Dhoya.' And at the same hour men say if any be abroad in the valleys they see a huge shadow rushing along the mountain.

1. NY: . . . somber . . . .
2. NY: . . . height . . .
2. L, NY: . . . rushed wildly down . . .
3. L, NY: . . . Dermot . . .
6. L, NY: . . . quicken berry.

14. NY: . . . eyes on the sea, and . . .
15. L, NY: . . . speed, and with a wild leap horse . . .
16. NY: . . . Western Deep.

# Notes to the Introduction

1. This remark is quoted in Joseph Hone, *W. B. Yeats: 1865–1939*, 2nd ed. (London, 1965), p. 58, and Norman Jeffares, *W. B. Yeats: Man and Poet*, 2nd ed. (London, 1962), p. 63. Both Hone and Jeffares, however, apparently place the date of the remark in 1888; this date is not in accord with the references to *Dhoya* in Yeats's letters.

2. *The Letters of W. B. Yeats*, ed. Allan Wade (London, 1954), p. 48.

3. "I myself have nothing to read you but 'Oisin,' 'Dhoya' and some few scraps, but have much to tell of." *Letters*, p. 55.

4. *Letters*, p. 56.

5. For information on the *Gael*, see *Letters*, p. 33, n. 3.

6. *W. B. Yeats: 1865–1939*, p. 58.

7. *Letters*, p. 58.

8. *Letters*, p. 66.

9. *Letters*, p. 77.

10. *Letters*, p. 81.

11. *Letters*, p. 92.

12. *Letters*, p. 94.

13. In a letter to Katharine Tynan on December 4, 1888, Yeats remarked that "my practice over *Sherman* has made my prose come much more easily. I am now setting to work on an article on Todhunter's book." *Letters*, p. 95.

14. *Letters*, p. 123. Roger McHugh, in *W. B. Yeats: Letters to Katharine Tynan* (New York, 1953), p. 170, identifies "the hero" as John Sherman.

15. *Letters*, p. 157.

16. See *Letters*, p. 169, n. 2. Yeats may have decided in favor of *Dhoya* upon remembering that one of the stories in Lady Wilde's *Ancient Legends, Mystic Charms, and Superstitions of Ireland* (London, 1888), pp. 53–55, is called "The Midnight Ride." There is no resemblance between the two stories.

17. *Bibliography of the Writings of W. B. Yeats*, ed. Allan Wade, 2nd ed. (London, 1958), p. 22.

18. *Letters*, p. 168.

19. *Letters*, p. 170.

20. *Letters*, p. 180.

21. *Letters*, p. 188.

22. "*Belles Lettres*," *Westminster Review*, CXXXVII (1892), 225.

23. *Letters*, pp. 167, 181. Joseph Hone, in *W. B. Yeats: 1865–1939*, p. 78, states that *John Sherman and Dhoya* "earned £40 for the author."

24. *Bibliography*, p. 22. Yeats also commented that "Ballah is the town of Sligo where I lived as a child—a vague impression of it but I think a true one." The inscription is dated October, 1904.

25. *Letters*, p. 488.

26. The dust-jacket of the Macmillan edition of *Mythologies* (London, 1959) states that "*Mythologies* was the title W. B. Yeats gave to this collection of Irish stories of the supernatural and uncanny, based on country beliefs, traditions, and folk tales . . . ." Apparently, then, Yeats also selected the contents. Although *John Sherman* would have been out of place in the volume, the same cannot be said of *Dhoya*.

27. *Letters to the New Island by W. B. Yeats*, ed. Horace Reynolds (Cambridge, Mass., 1934), p. 107.

28. *Letters to the New Island*, p. 178.

29. Nicholas O'Kearney, "The Festivities at the House of Conan," *Transactions of the Ossianic Society*, II (1855), 23.

30. *Keating's History of Ireland*, ed. P. W. Joyce (Dublin, 1880), Book I, Part I, 69–71.

31. *Keating's History of Ireland*, Book I, Part I, 85–89.

32. *Keating's History of Ireland*, Book I, Part I, 127.

33. Douglas Hyde, *The Story of Early Gaelic Literature* (London, 1894), p. 62.

34. Douglas Hyde, *A Literary History of Ireland* (New York, 1899), p. 282.

35. *Letters to the New Island*, p. 178.

36. *The Wanderings of Oisin and Other Poems* (London, 1889), p. 283.

37. *Letters to the New Island*, p. 159.

38. "A General Introduction for my Work," *Essays and Introductions* (New York, 1961), p. 516.

39. Mrs. Sheelah Kirby, compiler of *The Yeats Country*, has kindly provided me with information about Yeats's use of the Sligo area in *John Sherman and Dhoya*.

For a description of "Pool Dhoya," see W. G. Wood-Martin, *History of Sligo, County and Town*, III (Dublin, 1892), 221, 226–27.

40. *Letters*, p. 51.

41. *History of Sligo*, I (Dublin, 1882), 70.

42. *History of Sligo*, I, 69–70.

43. *The Wind Among the Reeds* (New York & London, 1899), pp. 84–85.

44. *Letters*, p. 247.

45. *Old Celtic Romances*, trans. P. W. Joyce (London, 1879), p. 106.

The basic plot situation of *Dhoya* is also parallel to the story of King Eochaid, Edain, and Midhir in the *Book of the Dun Cow*. See Philip L. Marcus, "Possible Sources of Yeats's 'Dhoya,'" *Notes and Queries*, XIV (1965), 383–84.

46. *The Secret Rose* (London, 1897), pp. 138–39.

47. *Fairy and Folk Tales of the Irish Peasantry* (London, 1888), p. 81.

48. *Fairy and Folk Tales*, p. 61.

49. Standish Hayes O'Grady, "The Pursuit after Diarmuid and Grainne," *Transactions of the Ossianic Society*, III (1857), 144, n. 1. P. W. Joyce also supplied a note to this chess game between Finn and Oisin in the Diarmuid and Grainne story: "Chess-playing was one of the favourite amusements of the ancient Irish chiefs. The game is constantly mentioned in the very oldest Gaelic tales; as, for instance, in the 'Cattle-Spoil of Cooley,' in 'The Book of the Dun Cow' (A.D. 1100)." *Old Celtic Romances*, p. 415, n. 26. Compare the chess game in Yeats's *Deirdre*.

50. Ernest A. Boyd, *Ireland's Literary Renaissance* (New York, 1916), p. 167.

51. "Henley has written to me about *Sherman* and *Dhoya*. He likes them very much but likes 'Dhoya' best." *Letters*, p. 184.

52. *Letters*, p. 187.

53. *Letters*, p. 174. The "problems" Yeats mentions were primarily financial.

54. T. R. Henn, *The Lonely Tower: Studies in the Poetry of W. B. Yeats*, 2nd ed. (London, 1965), p. 337.

55. *The Variorum Edition of the Poems of W. B. Yeats*, ed. Peter Allt and Russell K. Alspach (New York, 1957), p. 637.

56. Richard Ellmann, *Yeats: The Man and the Masks* (New York, 1948), p. 78.

57. F. A. C. Wilson, *Yeats's Iconography* (London, 1960), p. 38.

58. "The Trembling of the Veil," *Autobiographies* (London, 1955), p. 194.

59. *Representative Irish Tales*, ed. W. B. Yeats (New York & London, 1891), I, 16–17.

60. *Letters*, pp. 94–95.

61. There are a number of possible meanings for "Inniscrewin." Professor Brendan P. O Hehir of the University of California at Berkeley has kindly provided me with the following analysis of the word: "As it stands it looks dubious to me. 'Innis'—that is to say *Inis*—means 'island.' Innisfree is *Inis Fraoigh*, 'Heather Island,' but if Inniscrewin is a real name some word has been distorted beyond recognition into 'crewin.' *Cruan* is an adjective meaning red or orange; *cruinn* (pronounced krin, however) an adjective meaning circular or complete. There is a Loughcrew in Meath: *Loch Craoibhe*, where *craoibhe* means 'branchy,' but I see no way to get that -in on the end. Cruninish is an island in Lough Erne in Co. Fermanagh (about 40 miles east of Sligo town) and is probably *crón inis* (copperbrown island). Finally, 'Inniscrewin' could be 'Crewinish' turned around, but with the median -in- syllable repeated. This would make sense if Yeats was somehow aware that 'Crewinish' meant 'branchy island'—an apt substitution for 'Inishfree,' 'heathery island'—but unfortunately garbled in the transposition."

The Placenames Commission of the Ordnance Survey Office in Dublin has suggested an alternative interpretation of "'Inniscrewin'": "In form Inniscrewin immediately suggests the town of Inishcrone in the west of co. Sligo on the shore of Killala Bay. Although some distance from Sligo town, this was and is a well-known holiday resort and would certainly have been known to Yeats, at least by name. The name derives from Irish *inis eiscir* (or, *eiscreash*) *abhann*, "the inis of the esker (=sand or gravel ridge) of the river.' There is now no island here and it seems more probable that *inis* in this case means a 'milking-place' or a 'river meadow.' One late 16th century form we have noted of the name, Inyschrewin, (*Fiants Eliz.*, No. 4560 [1584]), is very like the form used by Yeats. Although it does not seem that inis means 'island' in the case of Inishcrone, that would be the first meaning to spring to mind and Yeats may well have thought that it meant 'island' here as in many other cases of which he would be aware."

It is impossible to settle on a final meaning for "Inniscrewin." Although Yeats's Irish was secondhand, he may well have profited from the assistance of Douglas Hyde in substituting "Inniscrewin" for "Innisfree."

62. *Autobiographies*, p. 114.

63. *W. B. Yeats: Man and Poet*, p. 56.

64. *The Works of William Blake*, ed. Edwin John Ellis and William Butler Yeats (London, 1893), I, 259–60.

65. *The Celtic Twilight: Men and Women, Dhouls and Faeries* (London, 1893), p. 29. Compare the following from a letter to Katharine Tynan on March 9, 1889: "Hey ho, I wish I was out of London in order that I might see the world. Here one gets into one's minority among the people who are like one's self—mystical literary folk, and such like. Down at Sligo one sees the whole world in a day's walk, every man is a class. It is too small there for minorities." *Letters*, p. 116.

66. *Letters to the New Island*, pp. 164–65.

67. *Letters*, pp. 34, 61, 81, 82, and 115.

68. *Letters*, p. 60.

69. *Letters*, pp. 81–82.

70. *The Wanderings of Oisin*, p. 132.

71. *Letters to the New Island*, p. 76.

72. *Letters to the New Island*, pp. 137–38.

73. *Letters to the New Island*, pp. 103–4.

74. *Letters*, p. 51.

75. *Letters*, pp. 187–188.

76. *Letters*, p. 165.

77. *Autobiographies*, p. 472.

78. *Autobiographies*, p. 7.

79. *Autobiographies*, p. 49.

80. *Letters*, p. 30.

81. *Yeats: The Man and the Masks*, p. 79.

82. *Yeats: The Man and The Masks*, p. 155. One of the two poems was later revised and published as "He tells of the Perfect Beauty."

83. *W. B. Yeats: 1865–1939*, p. 21; *W. B. Yeats: Man and Poet*, p. 63.

84. *Letters*, pp. 99–100.

85. *Yeats: The Man and the Masks*, p. 79. Other critics who have noted the division of personality in the story include T. R. Henn, *The Lonely Tower*, p. 26, and Virginia Moore, *The Unicorn: William Butler Yeats's Search for Reality* (New York, 1954), pp. 184–85.

86. The terms "hope" and "memory" are connected with "poetry" throughout *John Sherman*. Cf. "On himself, on these moving figures, hope and memory fed like flames."

87. This contrast becomes more meaningful if we remember that the early novels of Paul Bourget—up to *Le Disciple* of 1889—were heavily naturalistic.

88. *Letters*, p. 92.

89. *Letters*, p. 180.

90. *Letters*, pp. 345–46.

91. *Ireland's Literary Renaissance*, p. 168.

92. *Letters*, pp. 165–166.

93. Edward Dowden, "The 'Interviewer' Abroad," *The Fortnightly Review*, L (1891), 731. Dowden does not review *John Sherman and Dhoya* but simply quotes a sentence from the novelette in a passing remark. In a letter to Father Matthew Russell in 1891, Yeats remarked that Dowden "told me he likes the story, that 'it is full of beautiful things' and 'very interesting' though not a strong and dramatic story in any way, nor of course was it [so] intended." *Letters*, p. 180.

94. *Bibliography*, p. 23.

95. *Letters*, pp. 485–86.

96. I am indebted to Professor Brendan P. O Hehir for the following analysis of *gluggerabunthaun:*

"To say what it literally means requires first its analysis into Irish words, and analysis unfortunately produces two disjunct possibilities. It is either *glagar a' buntáin* or *glagaire-buntán*. *Glagar* means primarily 'rattle' —the sound of rattling, a rattling sound. By figurative extension it means 'boasting,' 'prating.' *Glagaire* is anything that rattles—a toy rattle, an addled egg, a pod or husk containing loose seeds—and by figurative extension 'boaster,' 'prater.' *Bun* means 'bottom' in a generally neutral sense, but it can mean 'fundament' or 'anus.' *Bundún* means, among other things, a prolapsed anus or the prolapsed fundament of a fowl consequent upon egg-laying. *Buntán* can very readily appear as a dialect variation of *bundún*. The suffix -[t]an, however, often indicates, in a somewhat derogatory sense, a thing or person characterized by the attribute suggested by the word to which it is attached. *Buntán* therefore could mean a thing or person having a *bun;* it could also overlay *bundún*, so that possibly in some dialect a *buntán* might be say a goose with a prolapsed fundament. The first phrase above therefore might be interpreted as 'rattle of a prolapsed anus' or 'rattle of a person-with-a-prolapsed-anus'— 'rattle' possibly meaning 'boasting' in either case. The second phrase might be interpreted as 'person-with-a-rattling-arse' or 'rattle-arse' or 'rattle-prolapsed-fundament' or 'rattle-prolapsed-fundament-ist.' Throughout the notion of farting is perhaps not absent. If forced to a single interpretation I would say: 'An approximate translation would be 'empty-rattling-arse.' "

97. *Variorum Poems*, p. 778.

# Explanatory Notes to *John Sherman and Dhoya*

1. The reference here is to Nicholas O'Kearney's "The Festivities at the House of Conan," pp. 18–19. O'Kearney defines a "Ganconagh" as follows: "The Gean-cānach (love-talker) was another diminutive being of the same tribe, but, unlike the Luchryman, he personated love and idleness, and always appeared with a dudeen in his jaw in lonesome valleys, and it was his custom to make love to shepherdesses and milkmaids; and whoever was known to have ruined his fortune by devotion to the fair sex was said to have met a Geancanach. The dudeen, or ancient Irish tobacco pipe found in our rathes, &c., is still popularly called a Geancanach's pipe."

This definition is quoted in *Fairy and Folk Tales of the Irish Peasantry*, pp. 323–24, as part of the note on the Geancanach; Yeats attributes the note to Douglas Hyde. A shortened version of O'Kearney's description also appears in *Irish Fairy Tales* (London, 1892), pp. 227–28; the Geancanach is there placed in a list of "The Solitary Fairies."

2. As Virginia Moore has noted in *The Unicorn*, p. 215, "Yeats not only believed in astrology, he was himself an astrologer of sorts, able to set up and read horoscopes." Yeats's own horoscope showed "something notable from an astrological viewpoint: a grand trine in air, involving Sun, Uranus, and Saturn, and traditionally signifying good fortune in things of the mind. Yeats was an 'air man.' True, his Venus squares his Mars; but, according to tradition, this aspect would menace his affectional life ('being in love, and in no way lucky'), not put a quietus upon his career" (p. 216).

Notice also a letter to Florence Farr on October 7, 1907: "In any case a man with Saturn entering his second house by transit has to look out for bad times. Astrology grows more and more wonderful every day." *The Letters of W. B. Yeats*, ed. Allan Wade, p. 499.

3. The Moon-Sun dichotomy is likewise related to Yeats's astrological interests. Virginia Moore has pointed out that "Yeats's astrology filled

his poems with moonlight, and defined the Sun as objective, unmental, unvisionary, therefore 'embittered' " (*The Unicorn*, p. 217).

Yeats also learned something about this dichotomy from MacGregor Mathers. As he wrote in "The Trembling of the Veil," " 'Solar,' according to all that I learnt from Mathers, meant elaborate, full of artifice, rich, all that resembles the work of a goldsmith, whereas 'water' meant 'lunar,' and 'lunar' all that is simple, popular, traditional, emotional." *Autobiographies*, p. 371.

4. As noted in the Introduction, the character of Sherman is partially based on Yeats's cousin, Henry Middleton. Another description of Middleton is found in "Three Songs to the One Burden":

> My name is Henry Middleton
> I have a small demesne,
> A small forgotten house that's set
> On a storm-bitten green.
> I scrub its floors and make my bed,
> I cook and change my plate,
> The post and garden-boy alone
> Have keys to my old gate.

*Variorum Poems*, pp. 606–7.

5. Unfortunately, I have been unable to find the source of this allusion. As T. R. Henn has noted in *The Lonely Tower*, p. 148, n. 2, Yeats "seems to have collected unusual scraps of information at an early date." In a letter to Father Matthew Russell on July 5, 1888, Yeats commented that "in my search for matter I have come on much strange literature— notably a Dublin magazine of 1809 devoted to ghost stories and such like. I have looked through several histories of magic" (*Letters*, p. 79).

Actually, it is likely that Andrew Lang, Arthur Symons, or some other person skilled in French drew Yeats's attention to the "French writer on magic." Although Yeats studied for a time in a French class at William Morris's house, it is not thought that he ever attained anything approaching a mastery of the language. See Norman Jeffares, *W. B. Yeats: Man and Poet*, pp. 48–49.

6. In *The Lonely Tower*, p. 187, n. 1, Henn has pointed out the value of this passage in interpreting the poem "The Cat and the Moon." It might be added that cats occupy a special position in Irish legends. As O'Kearney noted in "The Festivities at the House of Conan," pp. 34–35, "cats were special objects of dread, if not of some kind of veneration, among the ancient Irish. We read of several persons, both male and female, who had been metamorphosed into cats; our story-tellers used to spin out long yarns concerning *droidheacht*, or druidical cats . . . ."

7. The reference here is to "The Voyage of Maildun," which Yeats would have read in *Old Celtic Romances*. In the episode entitled "The Isle of the Mystic Lake," Maildun and his companions observe an old eagle, accompanied by two younger ones, undergo a renewal of youth by bathing in the lake: "Meantime the old bird, after the others had left, continued to smooth and plume his feathers till evening; then, shaking his wings, he rose up, and flew three times round the island, as if to try his strength. And now the men observed that he had lost all the appearances of old age: his feathers were thick and glossy, his head was erect and his eye bright, and he flew with quite as much power and swiftness as the others" (p. 161).

8. In *The Lonely Tower*, p. 255, Henn has noted the parallel between this definition of poetry and the following passage from a letter to Dorothy

Wellesley on November 8, 1936: "On the other wall are drawings, paintings or photographs of paintings of friends & relatives, & three reproductions of pictures, Botticelli's 'Spring', Gustave Moreau's 'Women and Unicorns', Fragonard's 'Cup of Life', a beautiful young man and girl running with eager lips towards a cup held towards them by a winged form. The first & last sense, & the second mystery—the mystery that touches the genitals, a blurred touch through a curtain." *Letters on Poetry from W. B. Yeats to Dorothy Wellesley* (London, 1964), p. 100.

9. The cataract mentioned here is one of the waterfalls which drop from the slope of Ben Bulben into Glencar Lake near Sligo. As described by W. G. Wood-Martin in the *History of Sligo*, I, 85–86, "one of them is called in Irish *Sruth-an-ail-an-ard*, *i.e.*, the stream against the height, from the singular and deceptive appearance it presents of the reversal of the ordinary laws of hydrology. When the wind blows from one particular point, the water is either driven upwards and back against the mountain, or it is blown outwards from it in a sheet of spray like a pennant." Yeats may have had this waterfall in mind in "The Mountain Tomb": "The cataract smokes upon the mountain side" (*Variorum Poems*, p. 311).

To my knowledge there is no placename referring to the Sligo area which can be translated as "Gate of the Winds." However, Yeats may have been thinking of the older and incorrect derivation of "Ben Bulben" given by Sligo residents. As Wood-Martin noted, "at the period of the Ordnance Survey, it is stated that the country-people interpreted the name thus: *Bin*, a high peak, and *bulbin*, storms, *i.e.*, the peak of the storms" (*History of Sligo*, p. 85).

10. Though not quite identical in content, this passage is reminiscent of a section of Blake's *A Vision of the Last Judgment*: "Men are admitted into heaven not because they have curbed and governed their passions, but because they have cultivated their understanding. The treasures of heaven are not negations of passion, but realities of intellect, from which the passions emanate, uncurbed in their eternal glory. The fool shall not enter into heaven, let him be ever so holy. Holiness is not the price of entrance into heaven. Those who are cast out are all those who, having no passions of their own, because no intellect, have spent their lives in curbing and governing other people's by the various arts of poverty and cruelty of all kinds." *The Works of William Blake*, ed. Ellis and Yeats, I, 259–60. As noted in the Introduction, Yeats and Ellis began work on this edition in 1889.

11. William Blake completed two sets and several miscellaneous drawings in illustration of *Paradise Lost*. According to C. H. Collins Baker, *Catalogue of William Blake's Drawings and Paintings in the Huntington Library*, 2nd ed., rev. R. R. Wark (San Marino, 1957), p. 19, the collection of John Linnell contained a version of the illustration to Book IV generally entitled "Satan Watches Adam and Eve." Since Yeats had access to the Linnell Collection in preparing *The Works of William Blake*, the allusion here is doubtless to that particular plate.

For a good color reproduction of another version of the same drawing, see *Paradise Lost*, ed. Philip Hofer and John T. Winterich (New York, 1940), p. 90. The Linnell version is now in the National Gallery at Melbourne.

12. In *Swan and Shadow: Yeats's Dialogue with History* (Chapel Hill, 1964), p. 214, Thomas R. Whitaker has noted the parallel between Margaret's brooch and one of Blake's drawings to *For the Sexes: The*

*Gates of Paradise:* "A Blake engraving captioned 'I Want! 'I Want!' depicts a ladder leaning against the moon, a small figure at the base beginning its climb; Yeats's 'John Sherman' mentions a brooch in the form of 'a ladder leaning against the moon and a butterfly climbing up it.' Symbols of the soul's impossible ascent, they may have led Yeats to use here [in "Blood and the Moon"] the dying butterflies in the waste room atop Thoor Ballylee. . . ." Whitaker's remark, however, seems to ignore the humorous context of the brooch in *John Sherman*, already noted by Henn in *The Lonely Tower*, p. 165, n. 2.

The Blake engraving is reproduced in most modern editions, as, for example, *The Poetry and Prose of William Blake*, ed. David V. Erdman (New York, 1964), p. 261.

13. Yeats may have been thinking here of the opening lines of Blake's "Auguries of Innocence":

> To see a world in a grain of sand,
> And a heaven in a wild flower;
> Hold infinity in the palm of your hand,
> And eternity in an hour.

Ellis-Yeats, *The Works of William Blake*, III, 67 [for 76].

14. Mrs. Sheelah Kirby has suggested that the house mentioned here is probably the old Cummen House, some of the ruins of which can still be seen in Sligo. As Mrs. Kirby describes it, John Sherman's journey to Knocknarea (see next note) seems to have been outward by the lower road, which Yeats would often have walked with George Pollexfen; then down from the cairn by the Primrose Grange side; and finally home by the upper road, past Merville, which would bring him along by the old St. John's Rectory where Mary Carton lived.

15. The mountain referred to is Knocknarea near Sligo. As described by Sheelah Kirby in *The Yeats Country*, ed. Patrick Gallagher, 2nd ed. (Dublin, 1963), p. 26, "Maeve's Cairn is, of course, the great feature of Knocknarea, a mountain frequently mentioned by Yeats. The cairn, which is on the summit, is a monument to Queen Maeve of Connacht who lived in the first century of the Christian era. This warrior queen of almost two thousand years ago is well commemorated by this huge structure, which has a circumference of 630 feet at the base. The slope to the crown is 80 feet and the diameter of the cairn at the top is 100 feet. It is known in Irish as Miscaun Maedhbh."

Yeats found the reference to the "sacrifices to the moon" in a note in Wood-Martin's *History of Sligo:* "Charles O'Conor, of Blanagar, in one of his unpublished letters, states the Irish name of the hill to be *Cnoc-na-re*, the hill of the moon, and he conjectured that it was so called from the ancient inhabitants having performed their Neomenia, or devotions to the new moon, on the cairn on its summit. By nearly every other authority this hill is called *Cnoc-na-riagh*, the hill of the executions" (p. 18, n. 1).

16. Yeats is basing this name on the original derivation of Ballisadare, a town some five miles south of Sligo (Ballisadare Bay is also the southern part of Sligo Bay). According to P. W. Joyce, *The Origin and History of Irish Names of Places*, 2nd ed. (Dublin, 1870), pp. 460–61, "the beautiful rapid on the Owenmore river at Ballysadare in Sligo, has given name to the village. It was originally called Easdara (Assdara), the cataract of the oak; or according to an ancient legend, the cataract of the Red Dara, a Fomorian druid who was slain, there by Lewy of the long hand . . . . It afterwards took the name of *Baile-easa-dara* (Ballyassadarra: Four Mast.),

the town of Dara's cataract, which has been shortened to the present name."

17. For the variants in this poem as printed in *The Wanderings of Oisin and Other Poems*, p. 61, see the *Variorum Poems*, p. 723.

Richard J. Finneran is an instructor in English at New York University. He received his B.A. from New York University (1964) and his Ph.D. from the University of North Carolina (1968).

The manuscript was prepared for publication by Robert H. Tennenhouse. The book was designed by Richard Kinney. The type face for the text is Linotype Electra designed by W. A. Dwiggins in 1935. The display face, Deepdene, was designed by Frederic W. Goudy in 1929. The book is printed on S. D. Warren's Olde Style Antique paper and bound in Bancroft's Oxford cloth over boards. Manufactured in the United States of America.